HOW TO ~~WORKING~~ A COMIC

AN INSIDER'S GUIDE TO A CAREER IN STAND-UP COMEDY

DAVE SCHWENSEN

Keep Laughing...!!

BACK STAGE BOOKS

An imprint of Watson-Guptill Publications
New York

This book is dedicated to:
My father, Edward, for teaching me how to laugh.
My mother, Arlys, for her encouragement of my laughter.
My wife, Debbie, for her comedy routines that keep us laughing.
My son, Kevin, for laughing at my attempts to make him laugh.
My nephew, Blake, and niece, Brooke, for laughing with us.
And to my son, Paul, who makes me laugh.

Acknowledgments

This book would not have been possible without the guidance, advice, favors, encouragement, or the opportunity to just "hang around" with the following people. Some were responsible for my 'big breaks,' while others were extremely helpful in putting portions of this book, and my memories, together. There's no order of hierarchy to this list, (such as opening, feature and headliner), just a big "Thank You" from me for what you do so well.

Among the significant influences on my career at the Improv in Los Angeles, I especially thank Budd & Alix Friedman, Mark Lonow & JoAnne Astro, and Fran Cowen; among those of the New York City Improv I am very grateful to Silver Saunders and Chris Blitman.

Numerous others have been helpful to me in my professional life and in writing this book: Jeff Abraham, Kevin Allyn, Ted Bardy, Dave Becky, Joan Brandt, Jeff "Smiley" Burroughs, Harry Capehart, Kimberly Chaffin, Tim "Andre" Davis, Jeannie Emser, "Dr." Bob Ferrante, Felicia Fletcher, Lee Hurlands, Barry Katz, Debbie Keller, Nick Kostas, Mitch Kutash, Matt Labov, Ross Mark, Jim "Mio" Markland, Al Martin, Thom Mercadante, Rick Messina, Chris Murphy, Sarah Nye, Dale Ramsey, Ray Romano, Rory Rosegarten, Glen Schwartz, Bruce Smith, Bob & Marlene Stefani, Pat Sullivan, Pastor Bob Wang, Doug Wellman, and Pat Wilson. My special thanks to Howard Gollop, John G. Cole, and the staff at *The Morning Journal Newspaper* in Lorain, Ohio, for their support in my creative outlets and their permission to reprint material that was first published by them.

Finally, a gigantic THANK YOU to everyone interviewed or mentioned in this book. I am a major fan of you all and am thankful for the joy and laughter you bring into the world. You are very special people and I wish you continued success in whatever you do.

DAVE SCHWENSEN

Published in 1998 by Back Stage Books, an imprint of Watson-Guptill Publications, a division of VNU Business Media, Inc., 770 Broadway, New York, NY 10003
www.wgpub.com

Cover photo of the author courtesy of Norbert Wagner, Vermilion, Ohio.

Library of Congress Cataloging-in-Publication Data for this title can be obtained by writing to the Library of Congress, Washington, D.C. 20540

ISBN 0-8230-8814-6

Manufactured in the United States of America

5 6 7 8 9 / 10 09 08 07 06 05

Contents

Foreword

The hardest part of stand-up is realizing that nobody's funny when first starting out. Oh, yeah, they may have a good bit or a funny impression they do, but ask the working comics who have been around a while how they were in the beginning and they'll tell you, "Oh, I sucked."

Now, the way to make money in this business is discussed in this book in great detail. Many people will tell you many things that are all very helpful and important to know. And you should listen to them, but my advice will be simple and pure: To make money in this business, be funny.

I remember when I had first started doing comedy. I was standing at the bar at the Improv in New York City, and I asked one of the regular weekend comics—I think it was Max Alexander—how he started making a living at stand-up. He said, "Just keep at it. You'll be making thirty thousand a year before you know it."

I was confused. How would that happen? Then, as I did keep at it, I slowly understood his advice. The more I got onstage, the more money I would make. Not then, not at that time, but in the future. For the more I kept at it, the less I sucked.

Nothing is better for business than to be good. Your only business decision when starting out is to do your act it as often as you can. Take as many punches as you can onstage for free. It'll all pay off later. But for now, just get on to get on.

There are different shortcuts some people try—classes or workshops—but nothing teaches more than doing, and doing, and doing. It's not easy in the beginning, but it shouldn't be easy.

Now, not everyone is good, no matter how many times they go onstage. But those that are good enough to do stand-up for a living have to learn it, discover it, find it onstage. When you have found it and you've got something not too many people have, you've got an act that's good. Then smart business decisions will inevitably have to be made. But never stop honing, improving, working, getting better. That's your best bargaining chip. In this business, that's the way to make money. Just ask my wife, who has all of mine.

RAY ROMANO

PREFACE
Serious Laughter

Being a stand-up comic is a serious business, with a lot of laughs. Stand-up comedy has become a giant industry and a major source of talent for movies, television, radio, theater, night clubs, trade shows, conventions, military shows, benefits, special events, and many other venues where laughter is in demand. As a comedian, you'll find that the competition for jobs is fierce, but because the entertainment industry is continually looking for new talent, there is always the opportunity to be "discovered."

As part of the entertainment industry, you are involved in a *business*. If it were not a business, then tickets for movies and live performances would be free, cable television bills would be nonexistent, and entertainers would not be regular guests on *Lifestyles of the Rich and Famous*. Since the basic idea for any business is to have a product to market and sell for a profit, it's important to know that in the entertainment industry the product is—surprise!—entertainment.

As with many businesses, the competition within the stand-up industry continually raises the standards for success to new heights. In Part 1 of *How to Be a Working Comic,* we'll explore the business methods and strategies that will further *your* career as well as the craft of comedy. Along the way we'll collect some helpful insights from the comedians Dom Irrera, John Bowman, Jerry Diner, the Amazing Johnathan, Anita Wise, Cindy Eaton, Scott LaRose, and Rick Overton; manager Dave Rath; agent Roger Paul; and the founder of the Improv Comedy Club, Budd Friedman. Then, in Part 2, you'll find many of the same lessons echoed in my interviews with twelve comics who have met the industry's highest standards: Drew Carey, Carrot Top, Bobby Collins, Micky Dolenz, Jeff Dunham, Jeff Foxworthy, René Hicks, Reggie McFadden, Tom Rhodes, Rhonda Shear, Rondell Sheridan, and Tommy Smothers.

Becoming a talented performer should be your first goal when competing in the entertainment market. But to be a successful talented performer you also need an understanding of the business. For example, your major goal will be to get those who have the power to give you work to see your act.

Regularly employed stand-up comedians know they are a product that has to be marketed and represented in the best way possible. Their main selling point is always a good act, but a good business plan is the groundwork upon which their success is built. Successful comedians are made, not born; there's more to what you see than just talent and luck. It takes preparation, practical experience, and a knowledge of what the business expects of you. Auditions, agents, managers, club dates, television appearances, promotional materials, and your image can either work for or against you. Breaking into show business can be like banging your head against a wall, so it will help if you've prepared well and developed a thick skin.

Still, there is no reason to consider a career in comedy as all work and no play. If that were the case, you'd find many of today's performers avoiding the business aspects and entertaining on street corners or anywhere else they could vent their humor for spare change. True, street-corner comedy is one method used to perfect an act in front of a difficult crowd, but with a little ingenuity and creative promotion you may find much bigger rewards in clubs, television, and movies.

Stand-up comedians get into the business for many more reasons than I can list. Some seek fame and fortune, while others love to entertain. It can offer an escape from the regular 9-to-5 "grind." And even though stand-up comedy can be a fun way to make a living, for some it's an opportunity to express their opinions and share their experiences. Comedians may have beliefs and causes that they wish to bring to an audience's attention. They have to make sure they "make 'em laugh" in the process, or find themselves a gig on a lecture circuit instead.

Success breeds success. One job is the opening that could lead to another. The job *offstage* is the same in principle as the job onstage: Be creative, fun, and entertaining. Use your talent to promote your talent. First impressions to a talent booker or casting director are just as important as your opening joke is to an audience. Make sure it works, or you'll be fighting for their attention the rest of the way.

The road to becoming a successful comedian has never been known as an easy ride. As with any other business venture, the way will be bumpy, and the horizon will hold more than a few ups and downs. To help you on the journey, *How to Be a Working Comic* offers a lot of advice on the industry as well as on sharpening your talent and many helpful hints given by others who have taken this well-traveled road. You will soon have a good idea of what lies ahead of you.

Now, before we start, you should honestly answer a few questions:

1. Do you think you're funny?

2. Do your friends think you're funny?

3. Do you even have any friends?

4. How come you're not guest-starring on *Friends?*

5. Are you funnier than these questions?

If your *yes* answers to the above number more than the *no* or *I don't know* replies, then you're ready to turn the page!

YOUR
CAREER IN
STAND-UP
COMEDY

It's Show Business, Not Show Art

There's an old show-biz adage that says, "Either you've got it, or you don't." In this case, the word *It* could mean almost anything: Talent, looks, personality, intelligence, or luck would be good definitions. *It* could also be any combination of those, along with various quirks, traits, or countless other factors that can come into play and pull someone from obscurity into the spotlight of the entertainment world.

In comedy, *It* means the ability to provoke laughter. It is a sense of humor, of course, but also the gift of being funny to other people—or downright hilarious.

Comedy *It* can come from many different places. You can be born with *It*, as in "You're a born comedian!" You can practice *It*, as in "How do you get to Carnegie Hall? Practice, practice, practice!" (A quick acknowledgment of Henny Youngman and we'll continue without vaudevillian examples.) You can search for *It*, think of *It*, write *It*, or hire someone else to write *It* for you. But the only way you can prove *It* is by getting onstage.

Many comedians start out lacking a lot of *It*. They may have *It* at parties, at work, or in conversation, but when they step onstage to entertain a paying audience for the first time, they find themselves in an entirely different situation. *Stage experience*, then, is vitally important. The more time you spend performing on a stage, the closer you come to being a more seasoned, skillful, and successful comedian.

A Case of *It:* Dom Irrera

Dom Irrera has a lot of comedy *It*. With a natural ability to be as funny onstage as he is off, he combined his talent with good business sense and experience to have a great career as a stand-up comic.

"My first time was at a place called Just Jazz, in Philadelphia," he told me when I asked about his first attempt at stand-up comedy. "A woman in a class I was taking thought I was pretty funny, so she got me this thing. I was an actor, and I'd seen that stand-ups had a lot of notoriety instantly if they got onstage at the Improv and at other clubs. I knew I could do stand-up because I had done that kind of stuff in college, hosting shows, and I had already been onstage for years as an actor and improvisational performer. So I could always bail myself out.

"Now, I don't know what it's like to go from, say, working at IBM to auditioning at The Improv. I don't know what that transition's like, because I never had to do it."

It's no secret in the entertainment business that struggling performers are always looking for their "big break." As in the movies, they want Central Casting's version of the stereotypical producer with the big cigar to point to them and say, "Kid, you've got it!" I asked Irrera if he could single out his big break. When did he know he had *It?*

Comedian Dom Irrera.

"For me, psychologically, my break was appearing on *Star Search,*" he said, "because it flew me out to Los Angeles. I had a barrier in that I didn't want to go to L.A. until somebody flew me. So that helped, because then I started going into the clubs out there."

In the years following, Irrera has gone on to make numerous appearances on *The Tonight Show, The Late Show with David Letterman,* and just about every television program that features stand-up comedians. He's had three HBO Specials and hosted *Full Frontal Comedy* on the Showtime Network and Comedy Central's *Off-Sides.* With such solid credits, what advice would he give to someone thinking about a career in comedy?

"Talent is just one of the many things," he began. "It actually has to do with a lot of things. It definitely has to do with the way they handle business. [Comedian] Uncle Dirty used to say, 'It's show *business,* it's not show *art.*' And that's hard for a lot of people to swallow. You think, 'Well, if you're good you'll just get stuff.' That's not the way it works. Talent is involved up to a point. Everybody thinks because their cousin Neil's funny at the family picnic, that he should be a comedian. It's not that easy.

"I think people should not watch other comedians, but find out what's funny about themselves. If they're really talented, they'll be good. The ones who try to become comedians just by watching other comedians, they never have their own voice and are going to remain mediocre.

"We're all influenced by everything in our society, comedians included," he continued. "But some people obviously study other comedians and then try to duplicate what they do. Maybe once in a while somebody will slip through, but basically it's boring.

"You've got to be funny and get onstage before you can worry about the business. It's important to be good. You know and I know that there aren't really *that* many good comedians. Now, that doesn't mean there aren't a lot of comedians who can work, and videos and pictures can still be helpful to those guys. But really, really *good* comedians—can you name more than twenty?"

"What if you are good?" I asked him. "You think you've got It. What then?"

"Look and see which agents and managers seem to be handling people that you respect and are doing well. Try to hook up with them if you can. That's a weird dance," he explained, "because you don't want to be asking them to manage you. You hope it might work out where they ask if they can manage you. When you ask, then they've got the power."

Sounding more like an MBA candidate than a comedian, he said, "Right now, I book a lot of the clubs myself. I've gone back to that. There's a point where you absolutely need help, but I have so much of a history with some of these club owners that I know them better than any agent or manager would. But everybody's different. If you were a young act going with a manager, the manager would never let you do what I'm doing, booking myself sometimes and having the manager book you other times. Agents and managers normally would say, 'Hey, it's all or nothing!' For television and films you have to have an agent, but not for the clubs. . . .

"I'm pretty established in the clubs, so I don't really need to go through anyone else. If I were to go into Boston or New York, where I know the guys who book the clubs, I wouldn't need an agent, other than to make money deals for me. And I talk to the staff. If the staff says, 'This is the best Saturday night we've had. Thank you for paying my rent,' well, if that's true (the club owners might lie, but the bartender's not going to lie) that's how I figure out the money—just word of mouth and what other acts get.

"The acts do talk to each other," he said. "Club owners may say, 'I'll pay you this, but don't say anything.' The acts are gonna talk, especially an act who brags about money all the time!"

"So," I interrupted, "do you think of yourself as a businessman as well as a comedian?"

He answered, "I've become one, because I've learned to not be manipulated easily by club owners. Some will use their 'friendship' thing to manipulate you. I booked a club one time, and another owner got mad at me for working that room. I told him he didn't even have a club there! He said,

'Well, that guy's a back-stabber to me!' I said, 'Look, if you want to be upset, fine. But you can't be mad at me, because I'm just working.'

"It's very hard when you first do *The Tonight Show*," Irrera observed, "because everybody wants you to plug them; they all think they're responsible for your success. So I had *The Tonight Show* announce I started out in one place, and you can see me in another place on Saturday night. That's all the credits I had—the people who'd helped me. ("*The Tonight Show* producer was in the club's restaurant," he added, "and they brought him into the showroom to see me. The truth is, the waitresses at the Improv got me on the show!")

"I get a call from one of the club owners who's mad about the mention of the other place. I said I was trying to figure out how to get both names in! When he got nasty, I said, 'Here's the reality of this: The one club pays me, and you don't. If it weren't for the other place, I couldn't afford to work your place. If you want to pay me as much as they do, then we can talk.' Once I started talking money, that was it. Isn't *that* funny?"

Show *business*, not show *art*—it was a serious lesson in how *It* works.

"In my road experiences," he remarked, "I've been pretty lucky, because I never went on the road just for money—I also went on the road for fun. I've always looked at it as: 'This is my *life* too!' Maybe if I had no money or if my career wasn't going well, it would be a nightmare. Some poor guys have to drive eight hundred miles for $500, and, really, they just make their expenses. I've been fortunate."

"So you enjoy the whole life-style," I commented. "The business part and being a stand-up comedian?"

"Yeah, I love it," Irrera nodded. "I was talking to Jerry Seinfeld—we were really talking about girls, but then we started talking about comedy, which we hardly ever do—and I said, 'I'd want a television series if it were given to me, but I'd hate to give all this up right now. I'm having too much fun!'"

I guess that says it all. Either you've got it, or you don't—and you pursue it like a business.

The Rules of Comedy

Before we go further, it's very important to explain the Rules of Comedy. Through the years these Rules have become more apparent than ever. Any student of comedy, after viewing a number of different comedy shows on television or in a club, should already know the Rules by heart.

There are two Rules of Comedy. They are:

1. There are no Rules.

2. See Rule number 1.

If anyone ever tells you that there is a certain formula for writing jokes or a definite method for performing onstage, then that person does *not* know about comedy. Just assume that he (or she) does not know what he's talking about.

Of course, there will always be certain club standards, business policies, or government laws concerning what is acceptable for the medium in which you are performing, and you would be wise to follow them if you want success. For example, you can't curse on television unless it's on cable, and I've met more than one club booker who counts the number of times a certain four-letter word is said onstage. Include a more than generous use of their not-so-favorite word and you won't be on those bookers' roster of returning comics.

Remember that all performers are, or should be, individuals, and the business of their careers should be handled individually. Audiences and industry professionals (from now on that term includes managers, agents, casting directors, talent coordinators, talent bookers, producers, and writers) want to see you as an *original* whether you're onstage baring your soul for laughs and observing what life has shown you, or playing someone else, a character you've developed. Keep in mind that it's always your observations and your interpretations that constitute your act.

You must be an original to be truly successful at this business. In music, we've already had Al Jolson to the Spice Girls and beyond; we've heard it and, if we like it, we already own it. We're not in the market for a copy. It's the same in comedy. Give us something new, something unique to you, and we might buy it. Dare to be different. There are no specific guidelines, plans, maps, or rules to follow when it comes to making people laugh. Explore, observe, take a chance, be unpredictable.

Which reminds me of a story. . . .

A Case of Originality: John Bowman

Many nights, maybe too many, I've stood in the back of comedy clubs and watched acts I'd seen many times, maybe too many. Eventually, if you can stand up to the repetition, it's possible to learn quite a few of the comedians' routines by heart. Sometimes it's almost a sporting event between comics to stand offstage and quote someone's act verbatim while they're performing (usually late at night when audiences are small). I've seen comics get onstage to joke with national headliners and do the star's act right along with them word-for-word, with all the accents and pauses perfectly in unison. It's usually very funny, but it also proves that some rely too much on the old "if it ain't broke, why fix it" theory.

But some comedians are completely unpredictable. They either count on the audience to give their act a direction, or have enough material or characters they can use to keep their shows fresh and themselves interested. It's fun to see them more than a couple of times.

One act who never seems to do what's expected of him during a show is the former host of MTV's *Comikazi* and a *Tonight Show* guest, John Bowman. It's almost impossible to describe what his shows are going to be like.

Not too long ago, when I was previewing his act for a local newspaper, I wrote a description of some of the funny characters I knew he would do during his show.

There was country singer Slim Bowman, Jean Claude "the Amazing Hypnotist," and the Party Animal, whose misuse of a Detroit Tigers athletic jacket would transform Bowman into a hyper-freak who immediately becomes the center of attention no matter where he is.

Then I attended his show. Funny, wild, and extremely entertaining—but there was one major difference between that night and what I had written: No characters! It was Bowman being Bowman for an evening of hilarious personal experiences and stories. This was great for the audience, but bad for my reputation as a journalist.

During his next visit, I decided to give myself a better chance at an educated guess. I stopped by the club where he was performing to get a handle on what Mr. Bowman might be doing during his current shows *before* I wrote my column.

As soon as he appeared onstage, he began ruining my preconceived notions by talking about some of his latest misadventures. Then he took a couple of walks through the crowd to see what they might have on their minds. Between waves of laughter, my earlier column was again burning a hole in my brain. How was I supposed to report to readers what to expect if the headliner wasn't sure himself? Who did he think I was, Kreskin?

Suddenly, there was a flash of Jean Claude, but Bowman quickly shifted gears and an imitation of Ike Turner took over. Finally, after some hilarious advice about what *not* to do for love, justice was served when Slim Bowman approached the microphone and serenaded us with his latest country offering.

Still, being unpredictable makes it hard to place a comedian in any category. A show from John Bowman, and other acts who defy set descriptions, will contain just about anything and everything.

After his performance, I caught up with Bowman in the club's dressing room and confronted him about my dilemma. "Every time I see you, you have a different act," I scolded him. "So many other comics do the same performance for every show. Is it this variety that has made you successful?"

"I suppose that's a part of it," he said. "People do recognize that I constantly throw things out, bring new things in. It's more like a weeding process. I don't throw hunks out just to get rid of it. I stop doing them because I get bored with it. I have to replace them with something else, so I find stuff that's topical, find the irony, and then just go with that. I'm always looking for stuff. It's like you're always working."

"I know one guy who claims he hasn't changed his act in over twenty years," I told him.

"I'd go crazy! It would be so boring. A lot of people have been coming up and asking to hear some of the older material, and I'll do it if I'm not bored with it anymore. I sometimes forget things for a long time. It's not purposely eliminated—I just forget them. Then I'll be onstage one night, something will remind me of a bit, and I'll do it again. It's fun because it's always with you. You just have to pull it out."

"If you saw something that interested you today," I asked him, "would you bring it into the act tonight?"

"Sure," he answered. "I do that all the time. That's one of my favorite things, to open the show with something that happened that day, something that everybody in the audience knows about, that's immediate. It sets them in a different frame of mind because they know that's something you hadn't had in your act for a while. Something really immediate may not be a huge joke, but it's funny because it's happening right here and now."

It was then I noticed Bowman eyeing the room. With his spur-of-the-moment work habits, I thought his wandering vision might be a sign of his constant need for change. Mentally he could be replacing the furniture, the fixtures, or even the interviewer. In case the latter was true, I quickly asked for any suggestions he might have for young comedians.

"If I say something during the day that surprises me, or if I read something and instantly see the absurdity of it, then . . . well, you're always working.

Every time you're talking to somebody, or reading something—you just think that way."

John Bowman is a performer whose comic material surrounds him whenever or wherever he might be. It is whatever is there for the taking.

So: There are no comedy rules. You may have to follow a few standards to perform on desired stages, but who or what you are is your decision to make. Find what interests you and go for it because, when all is said and done, there are no rules to break.

Defining Yourself

So much for rules. At this point I want to throw out

What kind of comedian are you? In his promotional material Tommy Sledge has defined his comic persona in a well-crafted and recognizable image.

a few hints concerning the behind-the-scenes work that will be taking up a large part of your comedy career time.

Working in the business end of comedy is very similar to putting together an act. Just as you must define your style of humor and make your act an example of it, you must define who you are and where you wish to go.

• Are you a stand-up expressing your own brand of humor?

• Do you appear as or portray a character?

• Are you part of a team or an improvisational group?

• Are you all of the above?

The answers to these questions are what you will need to get across to the industry professionals.

Some sound advice in this regard: *Never* copy someone else. (Hmm . . . sounds like a rule, and a good one, too.) Know the difference between being influenced by and plagiarizing another performer.

For example, everyone is influenced by something, somewhere along their course in life. You may drink diet cola because you were 'influenced' by an advertisement claiming it cuts calories. You know not to step in front of a moving car because you were 'influenced' by the knowledge of extreme pain. Well, many comedians, like other creative artists, can be influenced by the style of humor they enjoy. If you consider yourself to be more cerebral or sophisticated in your comedy tastes, then slapstick or general silliness may not be your cup of tea. On the other hand, if a good pratfall sets you off into hysterics, then your act will probably represent that.

In my travels, I've spoken with many comedians who are not afraid to point out their influences. George Carlin, Bill Cosby, and Richard Pryor are probably the most frequently mentioned, but the list hardly ends there. You may be watching an obscure comedy show on cable television and see an act that motivates you to get off the couch and try comedy. Maybe the comic was talking about his or her family and you came to the realization that your family is funnier. Perhaps this comic has a different slant on the world, which inspires you to share your individual outlook on life. Even a fun evening at a comedy club seeing a variety of acts might be all it takes to light the spark that will push you toward the spotlight.

What you never want to do is plagiarize another act. In other words, don't be a carbon copy of someone else. It could haunt you in more ways than one.

Comedians are very protective of their material. Sure, the more generous or business-minded ones may give or sell a joke to other comics if it doesn't fit into their act, but what they perform onstage is the basis of their careers and it's not for someone else to "steal" and profit from.

Beginners sometimes fall into the plagiarism trap because they don't understand what's expected from them when they first walk onstage. They know they need laughs, and some have gone to the extent of taking the plunge with material that has already been proven—by others, and there's the problem. I've attended audition nights where an act has performed a complete set memorized from a comedy star's latest album or video. I've seen newcomers read from printed sheets of paper that contained other comedians' best jokes which were available through the Internet. Others have copied mannerisms, dress, and vocal inflections to become almost a clone of their favorite comic.

Why bother? As I've said, if we already have one that works, why would we be shopping around for another?

You must never copy someone's act, because either you'll get sued and find yourself with a reputation as a comedy thief, or—maybe the less painful outcome—you'll get punched in the mouth that got you into that trouble.

If you're serious about your career, your act, and what you want to say, that shouldn't be a problem. A major point of this book is that to make it as a stand-up comic, you must be an original. I'll keep driving that point home and urging you to do the task of defining yourself. That's a big part of finding your original comic voice.

Before focusing on the business details of selling yourself as a comedian, it's important to understand what it is you're selling. The product is always your act. This includes its content and the way it is presented. There are plenty of great salespeople out there, but the most successful ones are those whose products deliver on their claims and advertising.

What kind of comedian are you? What do you plan to do onstage in front of an audience? What are you going to talk about? If someone were to ask you to describe your comedy act, how would you? These questions can only be answered by you.

> *"I went onstage and did George Carlin's and Steven Wright's jokes . . . and everybody said, 'You can't do that!' So it was back to the drawing board."*
>
> CARROT TOP

A comedy routine is something that is developed through experience and hard work. The successful comedians I've interviewed would never claim that their first time onstage was the best they had ever done, or that their goal was to continue doing the same act. The more they perform, the more they learn about themselves, the content and delivery of their material, and how the audience's reaction affects their performance. Eventually, they have a professional-level act.

As a stand-up comedian, you, too, will learn primarily through experience what you are best at. Are you great at one-liners? Do you tell jokes? Are you a storyteller? Do you have a quick enough mind to bounce insults off an audience? Are you a mimic or an impressionist? The list can go on forever, but the point is that you will discover your best talent only by performing.

Does this mean that you should walk onstage for your first performance with a clear and blank mind and hope the inspiration hits you when you grab the microphone? No way! The fact that you've put yourself into that position means you must have some ideas about what to say or do. That's the position you're starting from today.

There are comedians, by the way, who have started their careers based on a dare or a quick decision to perform. I've spoken with a few, and they claim it was the only way they could have done it the first time. They have a natural ability to be funny and are uninhibited enough to climb onto a stage and "wing it." It might never have happened if they had taken the time beforehand to think about it.

If that's your case, more power to you. But keep in mind that it's only the first of many big steps in your development as a performer.

> *"Friends dared me to go onstage. . . . I had never been in a comedy club until I went onstage. I started talking about my family, like I did at family gatherings, and people other than my friends were laughing."*
>
> RENÉ HICKS

If that's not your situation and you need a game plan before you put yourself at the mercy of an audience, then you must find your style and start to write some funny material. Suggestions in the following sections should help you start the mental processes flowing, help you form a basic act, and make you aware of your comedic talents. When you gather enough material that you think is ready to be performed, try it out on a few friends or family members. Get a "feel" for it, shape, and polish your act. Then find a club that has an amateur night, otherwise known as an open-mike night, and ask how much performance time they allow. Rehearse at home so you either know the material or have a good idea of what you plan to do with your allotted time onstage. When it's time for your first performance, do your best to be professional. Don't ever give people the chance to think you're wasting their time.

The Flaw in Instruction

I've run across plenty of books and classes that promote themselves as being able to teach you how to be a stand-up comedian, offering their "secrets," "techniques," and even "formulas" for developing an act. I assume no one would publish such books or teach the classes if they didn't believe they worked in some way. Comedy-writing classes and books are fine for those who feel the need for them, but I always caution the people in my workshops against following someone else's technique very closely. I've never met a successful comedian who used a "how-to" manual on joke-writing as a strict guide for his or her career. Once you've started working with your own individual creativity, the end result should be similar to that of any artist and will involve taking a chance. You may like the routine you create, but you won't know if other people will until you display it to them. The best comics just live with risk.

The major flaw in how-to lessons is that the laughsters-in-training will be following the same recommended methods. I've noticed that many of my former classmates from grade school have the same style of handwriting as myself. This is because we all had the same teacher and individuality was discouraged by the school's grading system. If you didn't conform and make the same loops with the required slant, you didn't pass to the next level.

If someone claims "there is only one path through the woods," then the believers will follow the same route. Safe, but not very interesting.

And having a successful career in stand-up comedy means doing everything *except* playing it safe.

Being original, creative, and individual is what puts certain performers in demand over the others. Admittedly, the overabundance of comedy shows on network and cable television gives many mediocre acts their chance in the spotlight. But which ones are remembered by the viewing audience? You can bet that the performer who has a different "loop" or slant on things will be the one discussed around the water cooler the next day.

When you study with people who claim they can teach you how to be a stand-up comedian, you run the risk of becoming only another copy of them. How many other performers have followed Instructor A's lessons? What's going to make you stand out if you're competing with his or her students for a job?

The last thing you want to do is follow someone's joke formula and become a clone. Create your own style of joke-writing based on your brand of humor. Be influenced by someone who's successful and whom you respect, but build upon your career influences while hanging onto your own individuality. Think of yourself as an artist. If you were a painter and wanted to put your work onto a canvas and display it for others to enjoy, would you buy a paint-by-the-numbers kit available to anyone, or would you let the artist in you create something unique? Your comedy act should be thought of in the same way.

A very successful comedian with many years in the business once gave me his "formula" for performing stand-up comedy. First, he would record his act on a cassette tape whenever he was trying out any new jokes. (Note: This is the only part of his lesson that I consider valid, and I'll discuss it later.) Next, he would listen to the tape and write out his presentation of the joke word-for-word, making notes about the audience's response to each line. Whatever lines did not get a positive reaction, or any reaction at all, he would eliminate.

He would then take the shortened version of the joke, try it in front of another audience, and repeat the process. Eventually, he would have his joke narrowed down to three lines which he could highlight with colored markers on a sheet of paper. Blue was for the "setup," yellow was for the "middle," and red was for the "punch line."

That was his style and what made his particular act work. But imagine how dull and monotonous a comedy show would be if all the performers followed the same technique. There would be no monologues, stories, slapstick, improvisation, audience participation, or anything else that can make someone's act unique. Put that kind of a restriction on a comedian such as Bill Cosby, and you would lose all the depth of his colorful characters and the stories detailing their hilarious experiences.

Therefore (that's quite an instructional term, isn't it?), I don't think it's wise to confine a creative talent with any "proven" techniques. *Self-expression* and *originality* are not terms I've made up. They are two main reasons why individuals have the need to perform and why some are more successful than others.

Now that I've spoken my mind and you're basking in this new-found freedom from the burdens of rules, how-to manuals, and opinionated instructors, consider the words of comedian Jerry Diner:

> If you are driven to do stand-up comedy, the force within you is a simple one. Find your own voice and your own material will come. It takes time, so prepare yourself for the marathon of a lifetime, because this is no fifty-yard dash.
>
> Enjoy all sorts of comedy, but don't have any idols. Otherwise, you'll spend your time trying to play down all the similarities. Your voice is the only one for you and is your truth. Search for it and enjoy it—and see that all the stand-up greats have found and are always working on theirs.

In the next chapter, I'll give you a few hints that I think will aid you in mining your individual creativity and developing an act.

Think Funny

Everyone has a perspective on what's funny and what's not. Anita Wise had these words of advice:

> One of the most interesting things that you can do is to analyze the people that you think are the masters, the ones that make you laugh the most. How did they do that? Analyze what specifically about their jokes makes you laugh. Dissect them. Sometimes it's not so apparent. You just say, "Well . . . it's funny!" But if you can get to the guts of the joke and why, on a technical basis, it works, you deepen your understanding of how to make people laugh. And yourself laugh. It helps you tap into your own sense of humor.

Strong advice for a future working comic: Analyze the masters' humor. Then find and develop your own.

There are probably many reasons why you've decided to perform stand-up comedy, and I would suspect that one of them is because you think you're funny. You have mannerisms, talents, or an ability to describe certain observations or thoughts in a humorous way. This is, or will be, the foundation of your performances, and you need to make it as strong as possible.

Today, as an exercise, become a comedic observer and reporter of your everyday life. Look at everything, including people, places, situations, the media, politics—any and everything, and try to find your version of its obvious or hidden humor. It's an old saying that "People can find humor in anything," and this exercise will keep you in tune with your comedy mind, while also helping to determine the substance of your act. It will make you more aware of what you think is funny.

For example, a situation can appear in many different ways to many different people. Now get ready, because I'm going to do it again with another old saying: "Every picture tells a story." That picture can be anything you see or experience. What we're interested in is what story the picture tells *you*. What you want to discover is how *you* perceive it. A painting of a waterfall could remind one person of nature in its purest form, while another might imagine a nuclear waste dump releasing chemicals just upstream. Either way, it doesn't matter what the story or thought is, as long as you follow your way of thinking and look for the humor.

Here's another exercise: The next time you're watching television, turn off the sound and imagine what you think is being said. Observe a situation and decide what you think is actually happening.

None of this needs to go into your act—at least, that's not what I'm recommending, even though it could happen. These are only meant to be exercises to sharpen your humor and keep you aware of what you're attracted to, but they could become ongoing disciplines as you develop as a comic.

Be Yourself, Be Different, Be Amazing

It's safe to assume there is a wide range of things that people think is funny. Some may think a pie in the face is stupid, while others may roll on the floor laughing. That there are so many diverse comics making a living proves that there is an audience for just about anything that can be said or done.

Anything? Don't think I'm exaggerating.

"Amazing" is not a word I use often, but there's a certain comedian/magician who has become an international headliner I do call amazing. He's unlike any act you've ever seen. Imagine a magician who is not quite sure he'll survive unscathed. One mistake with a knife could send a finger or hand sliding off the stage, or the misuse of a blunt instrument might cause him, or an audience volunteer, to visit the Outer Limits for a few moments.

Dangerous? Sick? Try amazing and hysterical, especially when the Amazing Johnathan ignores the blood-gushing wounds and follows the old "show must go on" motto. One of the first tricks I'd ever seen him do involved string and about a dozen razor blades that he stuffed into his mouth one by one. He succeeded in tying them all together, but the local blood bank seemed to miss a large donation while the audience screamed with horror and laughter. It was, well, amazing.

"Everything in my current show is new," he said over the crackling of a cell phone. "I've been doing more theaters, so I had to expand. I've added lasers

The Amazing Johnathan.

> ## *"We're going right back to the house, the home, relationships . . . It makes people feel secure."*
>
> BOBBY COLLINS

and special-effects lighting. I really dressed the show up and gave it some trimmings."

"I bring the whole show when I'm on tour," he continued. "I've got a sound-and-lights man who comes in early and sets everything up. It's fun, but traveling with it is a nightmare. I went from two duffel bags to anvil cases. It's like a rock 'n' roll traveling show, but it's worth it in the end."

I mentioned the first time I'd seen him pulling the razor blades from his mouth.

"The tricks are a little bloodier now," he replied. "Much to the dismay of my mom. There are always going to be some people who like the cute stuff. Not so gory. I got a little torn between them, but everything I write now tends to be sick. That's what I can write real quick."

The Amazing Johnathan has used his warped humor to move successfully into the big-time comedy circuit, which includes the MGM Grand, in Las Vegas, and the Reno Hilton. And Walt Disney World grabbed him for their spectacular Halloween show. "I never thought I'd be doing my show for Disney," he declared. "I just cashed a check with Mickey Mouse on it! What were they thinking of when they hired me? They told me I could bleed all I want, just don't say any bad words. They like the blood, so I designed a whole show for them. Went down there and had a blast."

The Amazing Johnathan also has a different outlook when it comes to the business of comedy. "My advice to young comedians is to stay away from straight, generic, suit-and-tie, talking-about-the-difference-between-dogs-and-cats kind of stand-up. That's not what's happening right now. Go to the toy store. Props, props, props!"

The moral of the story is as clear as a performance by The Amazing Johnathan is blood, sweat, and tears of laughter: It's up to the performer to develop his or her own humor and use it in a creative way to attract, entertain, or amaze an audience.

> ## *"There are always going to be some people who like the cute stuff. Not so gory. I got a little torn between them, but everything I write now tends to be sick."*
>
> THE AMAZING JOHNATHAN

You may find yourself more comfortable in life's "cute" situations, or you may discover that you gravitate toward a "dark" side that you could develop when writing your act. A comedian such as Bobby Collins might relate better to his children, their shared view on life, and the situations it can get him into at home. On the other hand, the Amazing Johnathan can see a household pair of scissors and envision himself as the star of his own "slasher movie." Rhonda Shear can make you feel as if you're a welcome guest in her living room, while Carrot Top would probably show and demonstrate everything in his living room, attic, and garage. It doesn't matter which road you choose as long as it works toward bringing out your individuality.

What to Write About

The question of what topics you're going to make people laugh about shouldn't be too difficult to answer if you've really opened your eyes and your mind and started to observe the world around you. Your next step, as you look and listen, is to keep notes on what you think is interesting, different and, most importantly, funny.

During our comedy workshops, I've had students get up onstage without any definite idea of what they are going to say. They haven't written any material and are looking for a starting point and guidelines. Some are nervous and even a bit embarrassed that they seem unprepared, but once they relax and begin to talk, the material quite often just comes out.

The best way to develop material by this method is through simple conversation. Get a friend to toss some questions at you about yourself. Expand on your answers a bit, and see what, or who, is interesting and amusing in your life.

If you are in a group setting, such as a comedy workshop, you can go further. We start out trying to make everyone more comfortable by opening with a few improvisational exercises. We play the captions game above using a few posters, and we act out skits with group members calling out suggestions for places, relationships, or situations for two onstage subjects (or victims, as we sometimes call them).

To get your mind working, the following are just a few examples of questions we've asked in our workshops. I won't list them all, but these should give you an idea of what to look for:

- What do you do for a living? Do you like doing it? Do you hate doing it? Are you the boss? If so, what are your employees like? If not, what is your boss like? What's it like doing what you do? Is it solitary or do you deal with a lot of people? What's your workday like? How do you feel when you get your paycheck? How do other people perceive your job? Can you imagine doing it forever? Did you go to school to get this job? What's annoying about this job? What's fun? What's stupid?

- Are you married or in a relationship? If so, what's your mate like? What does he/she they do for a living? What does he/she do that drives you crazy? What does he/she do that makes you laugh? What's your life like together? Apart? What interests do you share—or not share? Do you have any children? What are they like and what do they do that's funny or that makes you want to tear your hair out? Do you still have hair?

• Are you single? Why? Or why not? Do you date? Are you trying to find a date? Any good or bad experiences in the dating game? Do your friends try to fix you up with dates? What's good or bad about the results? Had any good relationships lately? How about some bad ones? What were they like?

Of course this can go on forever, with questions about your car, pets, travels, parties, parents, clothes, hobbies, comedy act. . . . You get the picture.

Examining yourself and your thoughts is a starting point. From there you can let your imagination and creativity roam.

The Writing Habit

This next bit of advice is essential: When you think of something funny that could work in your act, WRITE IT DOWN. Too often a good premise or punch line can be lost when you rely only on your memory. Buy a notebook and carry it with you wherever you go. Many comedians use one that can be easily kept in their pocket like a wallet. If you're serious about being funny, it can be just as valuable.

This is so vital I'll say it again: When you hear, see, or think of something that could be developed into comedy material, WRITE IT DOWN. This will ensure it from being lost in the everyday clutter that can fill your mind, or can save you the money you might need to spend on a memory course.

With a notebook you shouldn't lose your creative ideas just because you happen to be away from your writing desk when they spring to mind. With the competition in today's market, it's important that you don't waste prospective material that could further your career.

Keeping a notebook is also a great way to avoid the dreaded writer's block. Remember, you may be a comedic genius during conversations, but empty-headed when you sit down and attempt to write. So keep making notes.

Another way to keep track of your thoughts is with a tape recorder. Since I can't picture anyone wanting to lug around a huge boombox all day just to record their comic thoughts, I suggest a pocket-sized, voice-activated recorder that is easily used whenever an idea pops into your head.

The tape recorder can actually serve two purposes. One is to keep notes, and the other is to learn from your performances. I'll cover this second point later on.

Writing humorous material that you can use in your act should become a habit. Unlike a lot of habits, though, this is a habit you must work to develop. Writing has a way of being a task that is easily shrugged off. Therefore, my next bit of advice is to put aside some time to write your act.

You'll learn later on if disciplined writing is the best method for you—for most writers, it is. While it could develop that you're better off improvising your thoughts onstage, you may need to sit at a keyboard and punch it out word for word. You may be the type who writes best longhand on a pad at 3 A.M. You decide what is best for you. In the beginning, though, I suggest you practice the art of writing down your material according to a regular timetable. Doing this daily is both productive and commendable, but make your plans for when you feel most inspired. Just don't let that become a strategy for avoiding an important task.

Go through your notebook and work on your ideas. What made it funny? What could make it funnier? Make a joke or routine a part of the act you are trying to create only if you feel it's worthwhile. Don't force it. Remember the old expression "You had to have been there"? What might have been funny in a moment of inspiration ultimately might not work onstage.

Writing is a skill that develops the more it's done. Stay with it, keep jotting in that notebook, and then heighten that raw material at your desk. The contents of your notebook may be detailed jokes, but they may be only inspiration for jokes. Some may be useless in the end.

Because good comedy writers, and writers in general, know they're always working, it should be no surprise that many accumulate cassette tapes, notebooks, piles of scrap paper, matchbook covers, whatever, containing a word, an idea, or a line for a promising bit. It might be all the inspiration they need to sit down and write their next joke, enough of a premise to work it out onstage, or something they'll carry with them while searching for their next great thought on the subject.

As an example of writing from your hastily scribbled notes, let's take a subject that many people might already have an opinion about. How about the New York City subway system? For those of you who live near Manhattan or have ridden the trains during a visit, you already know what they're like. For everyone else, your only knowledge of the system is through what you've heard or read. It could be something you look forward to experiencing some day, or intend to avoid at all costs. I'm sure the mayor of New York would have a different report from the comics you see on late-night television, but let's assume you're searching for material about the subway and make a decision about your comic point of view.

Here's one that plays on the stereotypical reputation: *Fear.*

Comics and news reports seem to enjoy talking about the dangers of riding New York's subways. So, in your pocket notebook, you might have jotted down, "Subway—Fear."

What makes the subways so scary? Are they dangerous? Are you afraid of being mugged or robbed? Are you worried that the driver has fallen asleep? That the train might jump the tracks? That you'll get off at the wrong stop and never be heard from again? These are all worthy and fear-inducing topics for examination, but let's think differently from the commonly reported dangers that might be lurking around the corner. What about the other people who ride the subway? We've either witnessed or seen photos of some who sleep in the cars or generally look like they live in the stations. It's also not unusual to see entertainers performing for change, reformers handing out spiritual literature, or lost tourists reading their transit maps. In one *Seinfeld* episode, a businessman removed all his clothes and sat on the train reading his newspaper. It could be shocking to many, but just another "ho-hum" commute for the more experienced. It depends on your point of view.

There are also many others in the subway picture who might be just like you, actually using the trains to get from one place to another. You might want to only write "people" or "passengers" in your notebook and think about it a little longer.

Now that your thought process is continuing, what else have you noticed? Where exactly are you? Subway platforms are built between tracks, with the underground tunnels stretching out in different directions. Standing in the depths on one of these platforms, you might also see a newsstand or two, some benches to sit on, lots of advertisements, structural details, and the exits that lead to the street above. You're a comic observer, remember? So observe!

The subway also has rules (if you can believe it): You're not supposed to stand on the wrong side of a painted line that will put you too close to any oncoming trains. You're supposed to let any current riders off the train before you get on. Another rule that never seems too highly enforced is one posted throughout the system: "No Spitting."

Now, for the sake of our example, let's say this last observation strikes you as more joke-worthy than the others. Maybe or maybe not, but you see the signs all over. If someone crossed the painted line, they might be hit by a train. If they attempted to get in a car during rush hour while everyone else is hurrying to get off, they might be trampled. Scary. But what would happen if someone broke the highly visible posted law and spit? Would that person be in danger of being arrested? Or would you be in bigger danger if you happened to be in their way?

Now, I know this example could be getting a little repulsive to some of you, while others might be interested in that premise. It all depends on what side of the "cute" or "dark" line you happen to prefer. Still, maybe we can find a good (and different) laugh if we continue to explore the idea in some detail. Let's look at it from this angle: Subway, fear, and "No spitting."

What if someone actually obeyed the law and waited to get out of the subway before spitting? That could make the exit stairs a little more treacherous if you were walking up just as someone—you get where we're headed here. In fact, I think we may be close to a real joke. Let's try to put it into words:

> People say they're afraid of the New York subway. Not me. The subways don't scare me. What scares me is when I'm walking up the exit ramp and just about the time my head gets to street level I hear (make a real good "spit" noise). Now, that *really* scares me!

Admittedly, this joke doesn't fit the definition of sophisticated comedy material. But in one working comic's act it has been a proven laugh-getter, developed through observation and a good dose of creative (and fearful) imagination.

So look around you and observe what humor surrounds you in your everyday life.

Since your goal is to have a successful career as a comedian, it's eventually quite possible that you'll find yourself going through a lot of material and in need of more. Television appearances in particular make it necessary that comedians have a strong backlog of material. I don't know of any show that will buy the same act twice; most won't accept one that was performed earlier on a different program.

Imagine you're a guest on a top-rated talk show and your seven-minute set was so good that the host invites you back the next night. You'd better have another brilliant seven minutes ready, because their audiences are not going to laugh at the same jokes twice.

It's best to start organizing your writing habits *now*.

The Creative Process

During my experiences and in the workshops I teach, I've found many would-be performers looking for that earlier-mentioned easy ride to fame and fortune. What they most often ask is where they can hire someone else to write their routine. They claim they're not able to write funny material, and some resist the effort to even try. I always ask why they want to be a stand-up comedian. If they only want to perform with other people's thoughts and words, they should become actors.

Each time, they protest that most star comedians hire a staff of writers to prepare their material and most often point to Jay Leno and David Letterman as examples. What they should realize is that these performers were already established comedians before their careers took off at a pace where outside help was necessary. Try doing a different and successful comedy monologue five nights a week as these current late-night talk show hosts do, and you'll understand the need for a writing staff.

What you must keep in mind is that all these performers, for many years, had been thoroughly involved in an extended creative *process* developing their comic personas before they landed in their current high-profile positions in the industry. It was only then that they were able to hire writers who knew what to write for them. Yes, many acts today hire writers to help with material, but you must know who you are first, instead of letting someone else dictate that to you.

Putting together your act is an individual creative melding of your style along with what you think is funny. Your own personality, original ideas, performance technique, and stage experience will all go into forming an act that's unique to you. Beginning to create an act is work, but it's only as difficult as you make it. The important thing to understand is that it's a *process*.

I've encountered people who only want to be stand-up comedians because of the fame and fortune they think will be easy to obtain. They see acts in clubs and on television who make it all look effortless. The reason they think that way is because those successful comics have worked long and hard to make it look so easy.

Those of you looking for an easy pot of gold may as well find your receipt for this book, get your money back, and buy a few lottery tickets. Your chances are better. If you're willing to sacrifice your leisure time with family and friends or watching your favorite television show, then fasten your seat belts and continue. You're about to enter into the step-by-step process of putting together your comedy act and gaining the experience to make it successful.

By now you should have learned to become aware of your thoughts, conversations, and the life around you, using your notebook to keep track of your ideas. If you are in the habit of doing so, you have the basis of a comedy routine; the beginning stages of your act are right there in front of you. The hard part comes when you must edit, sift, change, refine, test, and re-test to make your act work. This will come through experience gained by performing in front of an audience.

What you need to do first is develop a five-minute comedy act. Five minutes is usually all the time a new performer will be allowed during a club's amateur night. Depending on the club's situation and location it could be more or less, but it's a good idea to have five well-prepared minutes, or remarkably good improvisational skills, before you walk onto a stage that first time.

At the beginning, find something concrete that you are confident enough to do in front of a group of people. Comedians tend to get burdened with labels (high-energy, low-energy, X-rated, ventriloquist, juggler, guitar act, and so on), but it's important starting out to get a handle on a specific style of performing. (Remember, what you decide now can change or be totally eliminated as you get more performing experience.) Many comedians start out by showcasing their best talent. They launched their stand-up careers playing guitars, juggling, singing, burping, or whatever it was they felt they did best. This got them onstage and allowed for development of a comedy routine. Some stayed with these talents, while others felt too restricted and moved slowly away from them.

I recently spoke with a comedian who started out as a "guitar act" and, through experience, decided he didn't want to use his instrument as a "crutch" anymore. His comedic observations and ad-libs were being limited by prewritten song parodies that he had been relying on during every show. He eventually started using the guitar less and less until, finally, he was taking it onstage but never using it. His "crutch" was only there for support, in case he felt it was needed for emergency situations—like when the audience wasn't laughing. Now he's developed such a strong act without the guitar that it never leaves his house, unless he simply feels like playing it that night.

If you have a talent that you do well, don't hesitate to use it to gain experience. Write jokes around it and about it and learn if that's the direction you want to proceed in. If it's not, you can eventually get rid of it.

Just don't forget, if you are demonstrating a talent, that you are preparing a comedy act. If you plan to sing serious songs, sing them after you've become a headliner in Las Vegas, or start auditioning in music clubs. Comedy audiences want to laugh.

Crafting Your Material

In one of my recent workshops, there was a woman who wanted to vent her anger about traffic and driving problems she had encountered. She stood onstage to perform her five-minute set, but nothing she said was funny. She was only complaining about certain incidents that were always followed by her simple question, "Why?"

"Why?!" I wanted to scream, "I don't know why! This is supposed to be stand-up comedy—not traffic court!"

Instead of screaming, when she finished I asked her where the humor was. She answered that she just thought people would relate to her problems. Her big problem was that no one in the class did so.

As a group, we examined her material and looked for the jokes. What was going on in the cars around her? What did the highway signs say? What was playing on her car radio? We went for details and observations. We exaggerated and lied. Of course, the truth can sometimes be very humorous, but when it's not, you do what you gotta do to make it funny. So we added things that never happened and subtracted things that did. We had people sunning themselves in the highway median, police arresting drivers for listening to bad music, and many other twisted and funny occurrences that supposedly happened during the woman's simple drive to the store. Pretty soon, she had the beginnings of a comedy act.

It's all a matter of using your imagination and looking for the joke.

If you've noticed, I didn't mention anything about a specific formula that we used to write jokes. I only told the woman and the rest of the group to be creative and think funny.

You're the creative one and you're the performer.

Whether you're relying on an inborn comic talent, or just a natural ability to stand and talk, you need to craft the act. That is, put your ideas in some type of order and work with them.

All performers do this in different ways, depending on where they are in their experience level. There are quite a few working comedians who would take out their pocket notebooks and throw them at me if I suggested they follow an outline when they get onstage. They pride themselves on observing an audience and making immediate decisions on where and how they're going to take them on a comedy ride. Others have told me they rely on a mental outline, especially when they're showcasing or auditioning, to guarantee that their act flows and the best material is not lost or forgotten. Whatever works for you will be decided as you gain that valuable stage experience and learn how your performing mind operates best.

I've seen most *beginning* comics appear more comfortable when they have a firm idea of what they're about to do. When I say to place your act in some kind of order, I mean to decide what material you will open your show with, what you would like to do after that, and, finally, what you are going to close with. In other words: *a beginning, a middle, and an end.*

You can flip-flop the order, add and subtract, or do whatever feels best as you gain experience. Right now you just want to get onstage, and having the confidence of knowing what you are about to do will help you get there.

How do you feel about the material when you are putting together an act? Does one topic lead nicely into another? Does it have a flow? You can put subjects or jokes in any order (no rules, remember?), but before your first few times onstage try deciding on what leads into what and when—exactly how you're going to do it. Develop it imagining how you would like to see it performed in a comedy club. It doesn't matter if you're telling a story, delivering one-line jokes, demonstrating a talent, doing a physical bit, impersonating, or even miming in silence. Whatever it may be, envision the whole act and give it form.

> *"There are times I think, 'I've got to do six minutes with a beginning, middle, and an end, and get off. Make it clean and crisp.' That's when industry people are there to see you."*
>
> SCOTT LAROSE

Start with a simple outline of what you plan to perform, or write it out as a monologue word for word. Then deliver it out loud. Is it funny? How can you make it funnier? Incidentally, there is no rule that says you must have a certain amount of laughs within a certain amount of minutes. It could be that every line of your act gets a laugh. Or you might have a wonderful story with a big punch line at the end.

The structure of your act will become more defined as you gain experience, but one idea that's important to remember as a performer—and as a business person (which we'll discuss in depth later)—is to always try to grab your audience's attention right from the start and end in a way that leaves them wanting more. Just opening the set with something that will win the best audience reaction can be a confidence-builder, too. So get a feel for what you think will earn the biggest laugh and plan to open your show with it. Then plan to close your show with a better one!

Practicing Your Delivery

After putting together your jokes, stories, opinions, or whatever else will make up your comedy routine, you must begin to practice it. Say it out loud. Do this in front of a mirror, while driving in your car, or wherever you can. Try it out in front of your friends. It's important to make it sound natural and conversational, *not* memorized.

Many acts do the same routine every night, but notice that the good ones make it seem as if they are saying it for the first time. Even your best "fire and brimstone" preachers and school lecturers have a good idea of what they will be talking about, even though it may seem they are making it up on the spot. The best make it look as if they are only having another conversation with a roomful of friends.

A skillful delivery means that you must know your act. It's not written in stone that it must be performed in exactly the same order or the same way each time. It may help you in feeling comfortable your first few times onstage

> *"In the very beginning, I felt a little better having a lot of my material memorized from stuff I wrote down."*
>
> RICK OVERTON

to deliver the material following your outline, but as you progress you will want to mentally be able to omit or add topics to please certain audiences.

The Ad-Libbed Act

If you plan to have enough confidence in your quick wit and ability to ad-lib or do improvisation onstage, your best training is just to do it. If you do your funniest thinking while standing on your feet, then I suggest you start performing as often as possible. I doubt the popular Don Rickles ever sat at a desk preparing his insults. He probably honed his skills by working off an audience. You may come prepared with lines or bits that you know will get laughs, but when you rely on an audience for your comedy act, you must be ready to go in the direction they lead you.

Improvisational ability is a rare talent and a skill, and the best way to develop it is by doing it. Still, you can take classes in improvisational techniques and learn exercises to develop your skills. Once you have the confidence to think on your feet, a whole new world can open up for you on the comedy stage. Beginning on page 92, you'll learn from Scott LaRose and Rick Overton, two of the most unpredictable comedians in the business, how they use that ability to make their shows funny and exciting for both themselves and their audiences every night.

Remember, no one knows what will happen the first time anyone steps onto a comedy stage. It could be glorious, or it could be a disaster. You'll only know by doing it. Either result should be an incentive to continue performing. If it was a great experience, you'll surely want to try it again. If it wasn't, you'll need to understand why, then work hard to make it successful. This may involve rewriting your act, changing the way it is presented, or making it clearer to an audience what you are trying to say or do. If you think you're funny, do what it takes to develop an act that proves it.

If you find you can entertain an audience for five minutes, try to do it for seven. Then ten. Once you feel confident you have a successful and entertaining fifteen- to twenty-minute comedy routine, you can begin to consider getting work as an opening act in local clubs and in venues on the road.

Jokes on Tape

Whenever you perform, tape your act. This allows you to hear exactly what you said and how the audience responded. You should always be looking for improvement, and there's no better way to do it than through a review of your performance.

Listen closely to the tape. Be honest with yourself and decide what worked and what didn't. As you continue the creation and development of your act, eliminate your weakest material. That way, you'll eventually have an act that has been proven to get a consistently good response from an audience.

Too often, I've seen comedians ad-lib a brilliant line or bit during a performance that they haven't taped. After leaving the stage they go through agony trying to remember exactly what it was they had said so it can become a regular part of their act. Sometimes it can be re-created, but many times it's lost forever. Don't take that chance. Tape your act.

Here's another hint I've heard so often that it's impossible for me to ignore. A popular theory says that a new joke or bit should be tried in front of three different audiences before it can be determined if it works or not. If it "bombs" all three times, drop it from the act. If it "kills" three times, it's a keeper. If the response is mixed, it might be worthwhile to continue its development until you determine if it adds or subtracts from your act. You have a better chance at making the right decisions when you tape your act.

To be a stand-up comic, you need to be funny in front of a paying audience. In the next chapter we'll look at how you can begin getting that crucial onstage experience.

4 Getting Onstage

That you've read this far means you're at least interested in the notion of standing on a comedy stage and entertaining an audience. That's good! It's important that you keep your desire intact and don't let any doubts creep into your laugh-infested mind, because there's plenty of work coming up.

To get started in a career in comedy, here's what you need:

1. Nerve.

2. An act.

3. A better act.

The first big challenge to overcome when performing stand-up comedy is to have enough nerve to get onstage for the first time. Once you accomplish that, you should find it easier each time you perform. Many successful comedians will attest that after their first laugh from an audience, they begin to look forward to performing as much as possible. But, in all honesty, there are plenty who never get over having a case of "the nerves" before a show. Some, however, claim that the adrenaline keeps them more mentally aware and helps their performances.

I've spoken with many beginning comics about their nerves, or lack of nerve, before climbing onstage for the first time in a comedy club. It's a frequent topic in my workshops and something I've paid careful attention to during most of the amateur nights and showcases I've organized or been a part of.

Everyone seems to have a different answer that helps them take that first step onto the stage. Desire alone might just do it. Some only want to get their initial experience behind them and continue moving forward. Others are of the mind-set that they're doing the audience, club owners, and the world a favor by sharing their humor with them. That's called "confidence," and even if they don't have the material to back it up the first time, it got them on the road to continue developing it in front of an audience.

I've listened to various theories used to calm nerves, and have even made up a few myself. The old standard that we've probably all heard while growing up is to imagine the audience sitting in their underwear. That never fails to get a good laugh when someone mentions it in our workshops but, honestly, I've never had any comics tell me that's what they've done.

Some look at the experience as similar to being at a party and the conversation has now moved to them. It's their turn to talk, and everyone is interested in what they might have to say. Of course, at a real party there aren't usually bright spotlights on you as you begin to speak, but by the time you realize that, it's probably too late to change your mind.

My advice is to always try and get your first laugh from the audience as soon as you can. It's another reason why I stress to beginners the importance of opening their set with something they feel will bring them their best audience reaction. Time and again, I've stood in the back of a comedy club with someone about to make their stage debut and listened to their doubts, worries, and about how much they're sweating and shaking at that moment. I've then seen the same person go up to the microphone, get a laugh from the audience, and visibly (at least to my eyes) relax. He or she may not appear to be the most comfortable person in the room, but it was enough of a confidence-builder to keep the ball rolling.

Later, the same person might tell me he or she was still a bundle of nerves the entire time, but never that the first laugh from the crowd wasn't a thrill. It's usually all the boost you need to keep getting up and working to get that same reaction throughout the entire set. That way, the experience of performing—like riding a bike, playing a sport, or getting comfortable with a job—becomes almost second nature, with a great incentive: As you improve, you'll look forward to doing it more.

Now, before you take your first steps, see if you can relate to any of the following statements. (No, this is not a pop-quiz—only a reality check.)

- I have no act.

- I have an act, but it's out of date.

- I'm not ready for anyone to see me yet.

> *"If I had been doing it a little bit longer, I probably would have never done it the way I did—I would have been afraid to! But when you've never done something before, you don't have that fear, and you just go with it."*
>
> RONDELL SHERIDAN

- I want to lose ten pounds before I go onstage.

- I need to hire a comic friend of mine to beef up my jokes.

- My day was so hectic, I'll wait until another time.

- Even if my workshop audience didn't like me, I'm *funny!*

I daresay most club bookers with amateur nights have heard all these flimsy statements and many more. If you can relate to any of them, it probably means that you are nervous because you do not really feel *prepared.*

As I've stressed earlier, moving into the world of comedy means being fully prepared. *Only* when you feel absolutely ready should you take the leap, because giving it your best shot means having confidence in what you are about to do. It is your best hedge against nervousness.

When you finally step in front of an audience, they'll be watching *you,* and, so long as they can laugh, they are willing to go in whatever direction *you* take them. *You* need to be the one in charge.

Open Mikes and Other Opportunities

Most comedy clubs have audition, or "open-mike," nights where newcomers get to sweat, work, fail, and succeed for free. The term *free* means that it doesn't cost you to perform, but you don't get paid either. Along with talent contests, where prizes are awarded to the best acts, these clubs are where most comedians start. Call your local clubs to find out their schedule and when you can perform.

Another way to keep an eye on where these "free" stages are located is by following the entertainment sections in your area's newspapers. I've seen open-mike nights advertised for coffee shops, bookstores, libraries, and lots of other places where you'd least expect to find them. Schools and various organizations also look at talent shows as fund-raising endeavors for which they might need a host or an original comedian to add some variety and laughs to a lineup of tap dancers, grunge bands, or Madonna-wannabes. For a prize, you might walk out with anything from cash to a potted plant, or an invitation to show up again next time. Whatever it may be, your main concern is the stage time. By gaining that, you've already won a small battle in a big war.

Another method to keep track of open mikes and contests is by staying involved. I'll mention this again later, but the more contacts you have within the comedy industry, the more you'll know about what's going on around you. Many comics I've worked with have struck up friendships just by being at the same clubs whenever there's an opportunity for them to perform. They share information, (and even rides), so they don't miss out on any chances to work out their acts on stage.

You can also make your own stage time by being creative. If a local club doesn't offer an open-mike night, you might ask if you could organize one for them. You could also arrange to bring a number of your friends as paying customers if you're allowed to perform a short set.

My own first experience in booking talent came when I approached the owner of a tavern with the idea of running a comedy show during a slow night. The comics I booked had to guarantee at least two customers who would pay a small cover charge and a two-drink minimum. The acts got to perform, the owner was happy to make money, and the customers had a fun night out.

Always remember that a club owner is in business to make a profit. Your best approach is to make it clear that a comedy evening would be as beneficial to him or her as it would be for your stage experience. Then work to make it a success.

Perform any chance you get. Hospitals, retirement homes, and even day-care centers may be interested in free entertainment. One method I mentioned earlier that is very popular in big cities is street-corner comedy. Quite a few acts I worked with in New York City would get together during an afternoon and take turns performing in a park or somewhere there was heavy pedestrian traffic. Occasionally they might have a small microphone and amplifier, or else they'd shout to gain a crowd's attention. Their experiences not only improved their acts immensely but also proved sometimes to be a great source of comedy material. And they'd make a few dollars after a good set if they passed around a hat.

In California, Michael Colyar became very well known from his afternoon performances on the Venice Beach boardwalk. In fact, when HBO filmed him in a special, they used the location and titled it *One Day Stand,* rather than *One Night Stand.*

A very famous comedian once told me how she gained valuable stage experience when there were no comedy clubs in her area. Each night she would drive to a number of different nightclubs that featured live music and would convince the owners to let her perform while the bands were on break. This went on for years, until she eventually developed an act that could not be ignored.

So, what are some of these clubs like that you'll be trying to perform in? They can be all

> *" I've gone all the way from doing book reports in elementary school, to Cub Scout banquets and church shows. Then in junior high school, I started doing some corporate functions. Then on into high school and college—it just kept going up and up."*
>
> *JEFF DUNHAM*

different shapes and sizes. The atmosphere of the room can be dictated by the usual types of audiences, staff, manager, or owner (hence the terms *tough room, tough house, great club,* and so on). Some comics may like the club, while others avoid it. They only way to find out is by going there and learning for yourself. I've been known to do that myself on occasion.

Exploring Local Clubs

Once, when I was sitting around watching one of the masterpieces of American cinema, *National Lampoon's Animal House,* I was suddenly struck with an idea: A road trip! You never know what awaits you beyond the next highway exit unless you check it out yourself. I looked in the newspaper for the address of a comedy club I had never visited, saw the name of a headliner I knew I enjoyed, and got in my car to get a firsthand look.

Until you've played a club space in front of an audience, you're not going to know what it's really like. About an hour into my road trip, I located a place that has the feel and appearance of what I think a comedy club should be. It didn't have the flashiness of the performance space that has become popular ever since television and films started looking at comedy clubs as a feeding ground for new talent. This place seated about a hundred paying and laughing customers and was intimate enough for those in the last row to feel a part of the show and those in front to see the acts sweat as they worked for laughs.

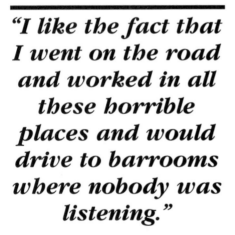

"I like the fact that I went on the road and worked in all these horrible places and would drive to barrooms where nobody was listening."

RHONDA SHEAR

You may find that some of the newer clubs are designed to make it seem as if you're at the theater. There are many acts who enjoy that atmosphere, but a working comic should always keep in mind the title of a famous song, "You Can't Always Get What You Want." Besides, in many of these "theatrical" clubs the design can actually separate the act from the audience too much.

The club I found was a great room in which to see a show, but tough for the comic. It reminded me of the type of venue that comedians speak of when they reminisce about "paying their dues." There were two separate levels the performer had to deal with. On the right, tables and chairs began at the edge of the stage and worked back, while on the left the audience was seated at a lower level. The setup was similar to entertaining in the middle of a split-level home.

The night's headliner, who had enough manic energy to destroy the room brick by brick if the audience didn't get his jokes, moaned about the layout. But then he went out, adjusted to it, and did a great job.

The moral of the story is that a good act will do what's necessary to make the show a success. Clubs, restaurants, hotels, bars, bowling alleys, pizza joints, banquet rooms, and just about any place looking for customers-all these types of businesses seem to have tried comedy at one time or another. No matter what atmosphere or layout these places present, your job as the comedian is to be funny. So you just have to get out there and find a place to entertain people. And enjoy yourself, too—it's the main reason you're there.

Your Home Club

The best performing space you can find is the one that will become your "home club," as many comedians like to call the comedy club where they first started, took their knocks, and got their experience. It's a place where the owners know them, have watched their growth, and will give them the opportunity to work on their acts.

Where you live will, most likely, dictate where your home club will be. Find one nearest you, buy a ticket, and watch a show. Ask the club's manager what the policy is concerning new performers. Ask some of the acts how they got booked there. If the club holds auditions or runs an open-mike night, become a regular visitor at those. Make yourself known and liked, and appreciate any time they give you on their stages.

If you have to call in advance or go through a lottery system to get a performing spot, play by the management's rules and go through the process. Even if you aren't scheduled for that night, go to the club and watch the other comics perform. Let the management know you're available in case someone they were counting on doesn't show up. I can't tell you how often that happened for me when booking acts and how thankful I was to see a familiar face in the room who was ready to go on at a moment's notice. Even if I knew the substitute had only five minutes' worth of material, he or she was helping me out by filling a void that would be left until the next act arrived.

Keep in mind that the better club management in this industry will usually remember these kinds of favors.

Another important trait is patience. You're most likely not going to become a regular performer at good club right away. There will probably always be someone with more experience (and better connections with the management) also waiting to do his or her act. Realize that, at one time, that other person was unknown also. Pay your dues patiently, be ready for any opportunity, and make the most of it. Never stop working to make your act the best it can be. When you get that performing spot, make them laugh, and chances are you'll be asked back.

Setting up a Frequency Pattern

Once you've begun performing, if you're serious about a career in comedy the most important thing to remember is to never *stop* performing. You must do it frequently to develop a rhythm. Like exercise, it gets easier the more you do it and harder to begin again after you've stopped.

Even established stars like Jay Leno and Jerry Seinfeld are known for appearing unannounced in clubs during their free moments to try out new material or just to stay sharp. (In their case, it's probably hard to quit doing a job that has become a habit.)

A month, or even a week, between sets is too long for a beginner. Too many young comedians drop out of the business because they never get comfortable performing. They don't develop a rhythm, and nerves from inexperience become a factor before each set. They then may find it a relief to delay future appearances and, eventually, disappear from the scene. This is especially true if their latest effort was somehow a disappointment.

Here's where the human nature factor enters in and where stage time becomes your most important ally. Every comic has off nights. Sometimes a bad show can't be helped. You have to remember what learning to ride a bicycle is like: If you fall down, you get right back on. You can make excuses if things don't work, but you'll do better just to persevere in getting stage experience, for it will increase the odds that you'll consistently do well.

Learning from Your Audience

The audience is always a big factor when you perform. Another reason to gain experience is so that you'll learn how to adjust to the room and be ready to deal with whatever the audience gives you.

If your act is mainly telling jokes or stories, you'll need to develop a talent for working off the crowd. If your strength is talking with the audience, you still must have some material prepared in case they don't respond. Or vice versa: Some of the most impressive performances I've seen have come when established monologue comedians were not getting their usual reaction from the crowd. Like shifting gears, they used their improvisational experience to involve the audience and brought them back into their material.

Exactly how you want the audience to perceive you will become more apparent as you gain experience through stage time. You'll begin to under-stand your comic persona better and also how to rewrite your act. You'll experience how it goes over in front of one live audience and then in front of a different one. Remember to use a small tape recorder to tape your act. Listen to the tapes so you can learn where the audience laughs and (gasp) where they don't. Make adjustments and go through the process again. Eventually, you'll polish your act.

A Classic Among Clubs

One club that's always been important to, and a goal for, many comedians is the Improv. Known as the granddaddy of all comedy clubs, the original New York City venue is where today's comedy-club scene started.

Many of today's top acts remember the small stage backed by the now-famous red-brick wall as the place where they paid their dues and hoped to catch the attention of founder and owner Budd Friedman. A true showcase club where comics are seldom asked to perform for more than twenty minutes, The Improv made a name for itself by highlighting established comics as well as the best newcomers. It became the place where the rest of the entertainment community goes to discover who's hot, and who's getting hotter, on the comedy scene. And it's known by millions who view the popular television show *A&E's An Evening at The Improv,* hosted by the monocled Friedman. You can't work in one of the many Improv clubs, or even be involved in the comedy business today, without hearing Friedman's name.

"Who were some of the comics who started out with you in the early days?" I asked him, as I mentally polished up my comedy act.

"The Improv started out for singers in Broadway shows after they finished work," Friedman said. "After about a year and a half we got a liquor license and—coincidentally, I'm sure—we started to get comedians hanging out. The earliest one was a guy named Dave Astor, who is a comic's comic. He was working the Blue Angel, which was the place to be in New York. All the

Budd Friedman and the author at a taping of A&E's An Evening at The Improv.

comics would go to see him, and after he finished work, he would bring them all over to the Improv.

"I remember him doing a version of Story Theater long before they did Story Theater in Chicago," he recalled. "We had one little microphone and he sat off to the side and told a story. It was acted out by Richard Pryor and Ron Carey, who was a waiter at the Improv. You know Ron, from *Barney Miller?* From there, just about everybody and his brother has performed on our stage."

Thinking back to my own days in New York, I remembered that an audition spot at The Improv was one of the most important breaks a new comic could have. It also could be one of the most nerve-racking as the comics put pressure on themselves to be accepted to the roster of acts. I asked him if they'd always had the audition process.

"No!" he laughed. "It was just a question of who showed up. And since I was the only club in the world, I was sort of a benign dictator. So if you came in, I might say, 'Okay, you can go on next . . . Oh, hey! I'm sorry. Robert Klein just came in. You can go on after him.' And then Rodney Dangerfield might show up—'Oh, I'm sorry. You'll have to go after Rodney.' Or, 'Richard Pryor just showed up, so. . . .' That's the way it would work."

"Did you look for anything in particular from these comedians before you put them on stage?" I asked—before he had a chance to bump *me* from my current spotlight. "Did you have a personal taste?"

He answered thoughtfully: "You know, the comics in those days were all so much more individualistic than they are today. Mostly because there were fewer. So you would never mistake David Frye for Robert Klein or Ron Carey. . . They were all unique, and they were all good."

Since The Improv was enjoying so much success in New York, it seemed it was only a matter of time before they went to Hollywood. They opened in Los Angeles in 1975.

"It was an immediate hit," he said. "We had Freddie Prinz, a big star on television. He was in the club almost every night. Everything went well, but then Freddie killed himself and the place burned down almost at the same time. It was a disastrous two years. Then we reopened, and Robin Williams and Andy Kaufman each did a night's benefit for me—I was able to charge $50 to $100 a ticket, something like that. So that put a few bucks in the pocket."

Many comics consider the Improv to be their home club and were encouraged by Budd and his staff. He acquired his reputation for finding new acts and pushing them to new heights, while also keeping the more established comics returning to his stage.

"If they're good, and I enjoy them, and the audience enjoys them, that's all that counts. What else do you want?" he reasoned.

"You gave a lot of comics their big breaks," I said carefully, knowing one line could make or break a great set. "How did they get on your good side?"

"By being good, for the most part. It's very hard to kiss my ass. You can kiss my ass and get on once, but you'd better deliver. Otherwise, it's not going to avail you anything."

Before Friedman could head off on another Improv Cruise, where passengers enjoy the comedy of his clubs as they sail the seas, I asked what the future holds for the Improv.

"We have the Improv Joke Machine coming out," he informed me, "which will be a coin-operated machine for bars and restaurants. You can put fifty cents in, or whatever it will be, and get a couple of jokes!"

Today, Improv clubs scattered throughout the country are still a home club for many; the list is always growing. But don't think you need to move to be near one. Look around your area and find your own "Improv" where you can get your start. After you do, keep in mind that audiences will always let you know what works and what doesn't. They are the best teacher you will ever have in comedy. In this business, stage experience should be treated as your best friend. And remember to keep in touch by visiting often.

5 Promoting Yourself

When it comes to furthering your career, there are successful ways to market yourself that you'll base on already proven methods. There are certain ways of doing business that are common for performers looking for work in the entertainment industry. Using your creativity, you can take some of these methods and create a promotional package that is all your own, including:

• your photo

• your résumé and biography

• your postcard

• your video

• your logo / address label

• your business card

These materials will take you to the next level. So read on.

The Photo

Most often referred to as *headshots,* photos have gotten to be pretty standard for almost any performing career. Actors, musicians, comedians, models, dog acts, whatever, all have photos of themselves, and nowadays videotapes of their acts are not uncommon—we'll get to those later.

In the world of entertainment, headshots are indispensable tools for the marketing of acts; your promotional 8 x 10-inch glossy photo is your calling card. It should announce who you are—that is, who are you on a comedy stage. If you can somehow add to that what *kind* of comic you are, then you're one step ahead of the pack. Members of the entertainment industry see many different types and styles of headshots. But the most commonly accepted headshot is a straight-on 8 x 10–inch photograph of the performer's face.

Among actors, the most popular shots are like those of Anita Wise and Bobby Collins, shown on the next page. These are formal photos shot by a professional in a studio. As simple as they are, both possess a vitality that is communicated in the performer's facial expression, especially through the eyes. It's essential to capture this vitality in any headshot you do.

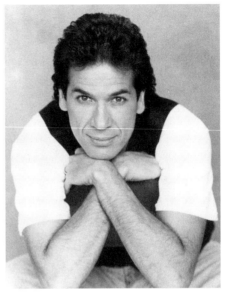

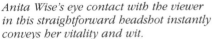

Anita Wise's eye contact with the viewer in this straightforward headshot instantly conveys her vitality and wit.

In his headshot comedian Bobby Collins projects the qualities that define him as both a comedian and an actor.

Some great informal headshots I've seen have been taken with the comic onstage, on the street, or in costume. Remember, this is comedy, so there are no rules—any bizarre approach you can think of is possible. Since the idea is to grab the attention of whoever is receiving your picture, who's to say what's best? If you're an angry comic, why look happy? If you're a happy comic, maybe you should look manic with joy. A lot of photographers recommend that women not wear earrings or necklaces to distract from their features, but if you want to be seen as a wealthy, high-class act, then why not show it? If you're raw-edged and cynical, snarl—don't come off as a choirboy. It's just another part of the business where your creativity should be put to use.

Though you have a lot of freedom here, there's no need to get carried away with zany ideas. If you're a happy-go-lucky comic, a smiling headshot is perfect. It can be a very simple process. Some comedians are determined to go to extremes to present an unforgettable look with their photos. It can work for or against them. Again, your guiding principle is this: Give the industry pros a strong idea of who or what you are onstage.

The important thing is to be remembered while also being honest and careful of how you promote yourself. A comic who once sent me a shot of himself as a big-time wrestler was actually mild on stage and couldn't live up to his image. His picture is what became the joke, and that's how he was remembered.

Variety comes into play when you know what you're going for. This is where your creativity can set you apart. It's a good idea not to let yourself be locked into just one look, especially since many of today's comedians also go on to act in films and television. If that's your goal, I've found it's important to have at least three separate headshots to submit for different projects: an upbeat one, a more serious-looking one, and another that's different from the first two. In the first case, it's usually accepted that smiling, energetic poses are best for crossing over into commercials and sitcoms. In the second, it's their dramatic, "actorly" qualities that comics have commonly shown in making themselves marketable for film roles. In the third photo, to be used on postcards and sent as a separate reminder of who you are, try for a more individualized pose.

Then again, with no written rules, the opposite can be just as acceptable, depending on the roles!

When considering a move into television and films, remember that good comedians can be specialty artists. They're supposed to be funny on a comedy club stage, but can demonstrate many different talents worthy of many different projects, and have various pictures to promote their talents. Robin Williams is an example of an exceptionally funny comedian who has moved into dramatic roles. I doubt he's using the same promotional pictures he carried when he first met the producers of *Mork and Mindy.*

> *"You have to spend money to make money. Spend some money on your 'press,' and do not keep using the same photo you've had for years. Have a bunch of different shots."*
>
> RHONDA SHEAR

A good headshot is also an accurate representation of how that person will look when he or she reports for a job. I once got a part in a commercial by submitting a clean-cut picture during an interview that had taken place months earlier. Since then, I had fallen back into my hippie–rock 'n' roll–save-money-on-a-haircut mode and neglected to cut my hair. The day of the taping, I walked into the wardrobe department and realized we had a problem when I was given a military uniform that didn't look quite authentic with a mane falling over the shoulders. The casting director made it very clear that she had hired the person in the picture and not the one who was currently trying to hide his excess hair under an army cap. Luckily, a pair of scissors solved the dilemma, but I had almost lost the job. I learned the hard way that you'd better give them what you're advertising.

Hiring a Photographer

Shop around, get prices, and hire a good professional photographer to take your shots. Find out what is included in the price—photographers vary on this.

It's important that the photographer work with you and give you the time you need to be relaxed and comfortable in front of the camera. Make an appointment to talk with the photographer and look at his or her portfolio before you schedule a session. Discuss your ideas and listen to the photographer's advice. Plan ahead about clothes, makeup, hair, and whatever else you feel is important for your headshot. Make sure you like the person who will be taking your pictures and his or her work.

After your session, go over the proofs with the photographer, your friends, other comedians, and any industry professionals who might be available to offer advice. Ask for their suggestions in determining which shots to use. You may have found the "best picture of you ever taken," but you might look like a bank president instead of a comedian. Listen to the responses you get, then make your decision.

The Résumé and Biography

Your promotional material should include a résumé and biography that you will send to bookers and other industry people with your headshot. Your résumé should include your name, telephone answering-service number, and any credits you think would improve your chances for employment. This can include classes and any special skills you may use in your act such as juggling, singing, underwater yodeling, or whatever.

I never recommend using your home phone number in any of your promo materials, because you can never be sure who might eventually come in contact with it. If a résumé or business card gets lost or thrown in the garbage, you may become the recipient of unwanted calls by someone who found it. This is a problem some comics have had in the past. And it's difficult to change your number when it's the only one you've been using for business. Phone services were developed to secure your privacy and to make sure your calls are answered. You decide who to call back.

List on your résumé where you've performed. Even if the venues are only on a local level, it's important to show that you have experience. As your career moves forward, you can replace little-known credits with more established clubs, colleges, corporate shows, television appearances, and concert dates.

For example, the following two résumés should give you a good idea of the credits of a beginner (the ambitious Johnny Biglaugh) and of someone who has quite a bit more experience (the famous Cindy HaHa).

Johnny has been working hard around his home in St. Paris, South Dakota, to get stage time. He's appeared at the three well-established comedy clubs, Rubin's House of Funny, Hysterical Inn, and the Funny Tree, and also listed three other "hot spots" where comedy shows might have been a one-time event or an occasional place to perform without pay. He generously volunteered his time for a few benefit shows and nonpaying lunch gigs, too, at two local colleges. Add to that the comedy workshops he's attended and a list of his special skills, and he has the beginnings of a résumé that will probably change and grow as he continues to work.

Cindy, on the other hand, is a working professional whose former "survival job" is nothing more than a memory. She's signed to a big management company and has been racking up television appearances that are very impressive, which is why they are listed at the top of her résumé. She's also had two film roles that she'd like booking agents and casting directors to be aware of, so they appear in an important spot immediately following the TV credits.

Cindy has played every major (and minor) club during her career but mentions only those with the best reputation. If people want to know more, they can always request an additional list. Cindy has also opened shows for some big-name stars, does well in the college market, and has an act that translates well for the corporate community. All that information can be learned with a quick scan of her résumé's headings and highlights, and it should be quite obvious to any booker whether Cindy has the experience for the job they're looking to fill.

Writing a good résumé takes care. The guiding principle is to make it clear to anyone giving it a quick read what your most impressive experience has been, with the most important credits displayed first. Look at the samples on pages 49 and 50 and you'll see this principle reflected in Johnny's and Cindy's résumés.

The biography is basically your chance to have the talent booker read about *you*. It's your story—who you are and, possibly, how and why you got involved in this business.

There are all different types of bios being circulated out there. Yours can be straightforward about the facts, or you can have some fun and be creative. You can write about:

• Your background (education or lack of it, skills, thoughts, or whatever you think might interest someone in *you*).

• Your family life and the region you grew up in

• How you got interested in comedy

• Your start in comedy

• Your comedy influences

• Your goals

JOHNNY BIGLAUGH

St. Paris, South Dakota

Phone: (555) 555–5555

COMEDY CLUBS

Fremont River Club   The Pilot House

Rubin's House of Funny   Michael's Pizza & Laughs

The Funny Tree   Hysterical Inn

BENEFITS

St. Paris Dog & Cat Hospital

Coins for Canines

Society for Free Television

COLLEGES & UNIVERSITIES

St. Paris Community College

Phil's University

WORKSHOPS

Maxwell's Marvelous Comedy Workshop

The Funny Tree Stand-Up Experience

SPECIAL SKILLS

Guitar / Harmonica / Paper on Comb / Juggling / Snake Charmer

A quick glance at a résumé should convey a comic's performing experience. Newcomer Johnny Biglaugh shows in this sample that he has made a strong start working in clubs near his home.

CINDY HAHA

The Major Management Company   Phone: 555–555–5555
111 Home Base Avenue   Fax: 555–555–5555
Big Hill, CA 11111

TELEVISION
The Big Evening Show   ABC
The Big Morning Show   NBC
The Big Afternoon Show   CBS
The Big Comedy Show   FOX
The Big Local Show   ZZZ

FILM
A Day at the Boat Show   Deep Mine Productions
It's a Fun, Fun, Fun, Fun Earth   Laugh Productions

COMEDY CLUBS*
Rubin's House of Funny   New York
Catch a Lotta Laughs   New York
The Funny Tree   Los Angeles
Hysterical Inn   Detroit
Fremont River Club   Miami
The Pilot House   Cleveland

OPENING ACT FOR
Artie Frazier   Happening Too   The Cools
The Note Tones   Frankie Jones   The Boise Sisters

COLLEGES & UNIVERSITIES
Forest University   Woods College   Treemont College
Surf College   Water University   Waxboard College
Burger State College   Pickle College   Cheese University

CORPORATE & BENEFIT PERFORMANCES*
Big Money Finances   Sue's Attorneys   U-Finance Car Dealers
Devil May Care Morticians   Couch's Potatoes   Skip's Vinyl Records

*Additional list available upon request

The more experienced Cindy HaHa is signed to a management company,
as reflected in her résumé, and she lists her important TV appearances first.
Of the many clubs she has played she includes only the best known.

- The type of material or act you perform

- Your best career highlights

- Some of the more outrageous things that have happened to you in your comedy career

- Some lines from your act that best describe you

- Anything and everything that would add to your reputation as a working comedian

It shouldn't be too long or self-indulgent (they know you think you're good—that's why you're sending your promotional package!). Just make it readable and entertaining.

For entertainers putting together their initial promotional package (or press kit, as it's also called), I've always suggested they limit their bio to a single page in length. If one or two paragraphs say everything you think is necessary, that's fine, because the idea is to keep it simple and convenient for anyone who might be reading it. (After you become a big star, you can write your autobiography, and we can all spend leisurely afternoons reading about the details of your life.) You may also find there are showcase applications, playbills (programs) for theaters and benefits, or an opportunity for advertising yourself where a bio is required to be no longer than 150 words, and sometimes less. So it's a good idea to have one version edited with that in mind, just in case you ever need it.

Once you reach higher levels of popularity, your bio will grow in length to cover all your career highlights. Major stars have publicists who send out biographies to promoters, television and radio stations, newspapers, and magazines wherever they may be performing, and these bios can be anywhere from one fact-filled page to a half-dozen or more. They might mention starring roles in sitcoms or films, complete with plot and character descriptions; awards and nominations; charitable projects; a performer's creation of a self-named comedy-club chain; and just about anything else that conveys that he or she is a star.

When first setting up your résumé and bio, you'll want to make it look as professional as you can. This is simple if you have a home computer or access to one. Play with different fonts and type sizes and make the total package visually attractive. Whatever you do, make it easy on the eye—it must never be difficult to read. Stay away from scribbling things on the printed-out sheet with pencil or crayon (believe it or not, I've seen both)—unless you're an artist and your talent helps convey who you are onstage.

Your name in bold letters at the top, followed by your phone service number—always important if your other material is misplaced and a booker is looking to find you—and, finally, the text, is a standard and acceptable form. If you have a logo, find a suitable place on the page for it.

Johnny Biglaugh

(555) 555–5555

Growing up in St. Paris, South Dakota, Johnny Biglaugh always found an audience for his offbeat brand of comedy. Encouraged by frustrated teachers and laughing classmates, he entered a local comedy club's amateur contest and walked away not only $50 richer, as the first-place winner, but also with a new career goal in mind: stand-up comedy.

His parents, a source of much of his comedy material, reacted swiftly. They wished him luck, made sure he graduated, and rented out his room to the first caller.

Johnny's comedy education has continued with return engagements at clubs throughout the state. With a unique talent for characters and improvisation, his performances have been described as off-center, thought-provoking, and funny. A recent benefit show he hosted for the Society for Free Television broke the previous year's record for donations—and he's already been asked to return!

Often called a cross between Jerry Lewis and Bill Cosby, his material touches on everything from family life and everyday situations to some of his more absurd observations about the world around us. Johnny Biglaugh only wants to make you laugh . . . and to be welcomed home again as an occasional overnight guest.

A sample biography for Johnny Biglaugh

M A N A G E M E N T

The Major Management Company Presents . . .

CINDY HAHA

Cindy HaHa, recently nominated for her second Comedy Award, has been headlining shows throughout the country for more than a decade. Her sharp, razor-like wit has brought her comparisons to Don Rickles and made her a favorite guest on *The Big Evening Show,* where she delivered the now-famous line to host Frankie Jones:

> "I'm not in it for the money, but your generous offer
> of a choice between soup and an eggroll is not gonna
> power my car!"

Her other TV appearances include *The Big Morning Show, The Big Afternoon Show,* and *The Big Comedy Show.*

A native of Newark, New Jersey, Cindy first made her mark in New York's comedy clubs, where she caught the attention of director Mike Mike at Deep Mine Productions, who cast her as Ginger in the hit film *A Day at the Boat Show.* Her hysterical performance earned her the part of a psychotic schoolteacher in Laugh Productions' latest movie, *It's a Fun, Fun, Fun, Fun Earth,* to be released early this fall.

Between film roles, headlining tours, and appearances in Las Vegas and Atlantic City, Cindy has found scarcely any time to enjoy her new home base, Los Angeles. During her few free moments, she enjoys writing scripts for a proposed self-named sitcom and searching for New York pizza.

THE MAJOR MANAGEMENT COMPANY • MELROSE AVENUE • LOS ANGELES, CA 90067
PHONE: 555-555-5555 • FAX: 555-555-5556

A sample biography for Cindy HaHa

There are different ways this can be presented. Actors are known for putting their résumés right on the back of their 8 x 10" headshots and handing it to casting directors. Comedians can do this also, with their bio and other material paper-clipped together with it, but they have the opportunity to be a little more flexible. A two-pocket folder always makes a nice presentation, with your picture on one side and your résumé, bio, letters of recommendation, newspaper clippings, and additional promotional material tucked into the other. Use a folder with a notch cut in it for your business card to fit into (on the inside), then paste a simple label with your name and service number on the cover, and you'll have the beginnings of a professional-looking promotional package.

The Postcard

An important word about postcards: They work. Some performers write them off as unnecessary, but I've known postcards to play a big part in helping someone remember a comic. If someone can give you a job and hasn't responded to your promotional material, it's no crime to occasionally send that person a postcard as a reminder that you're still available for work. A simple "hello" is one way to keep your face on a club owner's desk and your name fresh in a booker's mind.

My advice is that you maintain a mailing list of contacts, and any time you work or achieve something in the business, write a note about it on the back of your postcard and drop one in the mail to each of your contacts. Chances are it will make you recognizable even to those people you have never met.

There are many different methods to use when planning your postcards; again, the only limitation is your own creativity. Keep in mind that they are meant to be a simple reminder of who you are and how you can be reached. A headshot, a photo of you onstage, or one taken of you working in a theatrical or television project will do. Think of it as a large business card containing your face, telephone service number, and a short message that can be sent through the mail.

Postcards are a very important career tool and their value should never be underestimated. Cindy Eaton advises:

> As a comic, you've got to spend a lot of time writing—write, write, write, and when you've got some free time, write! It's also important to keep in touch with the folks you're doing business with. Postcards are a great way to say "hey" to everyone from bookers, agents, and casting directors to other comics. I use them most often to follow up after sending my tape and press package, to update my availabilities, and to thank people for their time. It's less costly than sending a letter, serves to connect your name and face in the mind of the receiver, and it's quick, both for the writer and the reader. And quick is good. Why? Because you need your time to write!

Comedian Cindy Eaton uses this postcard for her "follow-ups." (Photo courtesy of Tess Steinkolk)

Jerry Diner's postcard is a mini-version of his headshot. (Photo courtesy of Denna Brian)

The Video

In comedy, the most important part of your promotional package is a videotape of your act. A headshot might make your face recognizable, but a video is a better example of what you have to offer.

Videos have made life a lot easier for industry professionals while adding another mountain for the talent to climb. Videos are compact and convenient. They're delivered just like a headshot and can be watched at any time. They can be stacked and catalogued and instantly reviewed when looking for talent.

Every comedian who is serious about a career arranges to have a video made. Every industry professional serious about finding new talent watches videotapes. Of course, nothing beats a live performance in front of a live audience, but talent scouts can't possibly see every act in every club every night. The VCR is now an invaluable part of any office.

> *"It's all in the presentation. A video and picture is your calling card, now that video has become more important with the advent of VH-1, MTV and all these rock videos."*
>
> BOBBY COLLINS

Sometimes clubs and television shows book acts solely from watching a videotape. It's rare, but it happens. Usually, if they find the tape interesting, the booker will schedule a showcase to see the act perform live. Some road clubs must rely on tape because their locations don't allow that many acts to showcase.

A successful video has to be a good-quality tape that's easy to watch and listen to. It also has to grab viewers' attention right away and keep them eager to see more. Usually, the fast forward button is just a touch away and your viewers have a number of tapes to go through. The minute you lose them, chances are they'll speed through your act and only sample parts along the way. It's quite possible they could miss your best material and only stop at dreaded "dead air" periods.

All that's needed for a video that you'll submit as an introduction to you and your act, even for a television spot like *A&E's An Evening at The Improv* or *The Tonight Show,* is seven to ten minutes—make that seven to ten *solid* minutes—of *comedy.* Out-of-town comedy clubs usually want to see twenty minutes of material for opening or middle acts.

Like headshots, videos are best made by professionals. They normally get better results than a friend with a video camera in the back of a club. Their lighting know-how, sound equipment, and ability to follow you smoothly onstage make a difference. Ask around and get recommendations from working comedians to find the best person to do your tape.

Watch comedians on television, and study other comics' tapes. What do you find in the visual presentation that you like? Do you wish there were an occasional close-up? Are there parts of the act when the entire stage is being used? How well were these taped? It's important to know what you want and to communicate your ideas to the person filming your set.

Ideally, you want a good audience for your taping. That's usually hard to control, but there are ways you can get the odds in your favor. Explain to a club booker that you want to make a video of your act and would like to do it in his or her club. If the booker knows you, likes your act, and schedules you to perform, do the taping on the club's high-attendance night and hope for a good response. Even if you're not on the schedule, you might be allowed to do seven minutes for no pay. Then invite your friends, relatives, and anyone else who will laugh during your set.

You call this cheating? Well . . . maybe it is, but it's your career that you are trying to further, and it can help you in at least three different ways:

1. It could give you extra incentive for a better performance because people you know are watching.

2. You might have a performance slot where the evening's audience would usually be distracted. Menus, table service, checks, or conversations are often obstacles to work through when performing live. People laughing at your act might draw the rest of the audience to pay more attention.

3. Talent bookers watching your tape will hear the audience's reaction (because it's a good-quality tape, right?) and decide to showcase you because of it. Even if they don't personally like your material, their success is based on pleasing paying customers. If it sounds like paying customers are enjoying your show . . . well, you figure it out!

Talent bookers put a lot of weight on point number 3. How many times have you heard other comics complaining about "hacks" who get all the work, even though they're convinced their own material is more funny, thoughtful, and relevant? The reason might be that the audience is laughing harder at the so-called hack. After all, laughter's not a new factor in the scheduling decisions; a club owner or booker must take into account the audience's reaction and the number of seats an act can fill.

Make sure your tape is entertaining (as in funny) and an honest representation of what you do onstage. Don't use any effects or techniques for the video that you'd be unable to reproduce on television shows or in the clubs you are submitting it to. I occasionally receive videos in which locations, sets, and costume changes are integral parts of someone's act. Even if it was excellent comedy, it couldn't possibly be presented with the same results on a comedy club stage. Need I say that those acts wouldn't get the booking?

Once you've taped your set, remember to keep any editing done on it to a minimum. *No* editing is best. If you've done a solid show that was successful, leave it alone and present it that way. But if there are parts that didn't work and make you look bad, then it's in your best interest to take them out. The important thing here is to be careful about how this is done. When you watch a video that's been spliced and cut into an uneven flow, it's only natural to wonder why so much has been left out. People might conclude that you have an hour show, but only seven minutes of it is funny.

Make sure the person watching your tape can reach you. Don't take a chance that your personal information on a headshot or cover letter are enough. More often than not, your video will be separated from the rest of your promotional material and viewed later. Always label your videotapes with your name and a phone number. If you already have an agent or manager, contact information for them should appear on the label along with your name.

A terrific video will be an important asset when it comes to breaking into television, which is covered later, in Chapter 9.

Logo / Address Label

Getting your promotional material noticed is another way you can assert your individuality. Learn to be creative with the standard practices. In contacting industry professionals, some acts prefer to deliver their headshots and videos personally. But be prepared: If you're lucky you might get an immediate audition, and if you're not so lucky the distraction you cause by appearing without an appointment could bury you in Bad-First-Impression-Land.

If your winning personality doesn't get you through the door, or if you're 2,000 miles away, who says you can't mail your material in a uniquely styled or colored envelope? How about a personal logo as part of your mailing return address? Make it stand out. You can call the booking office in a few days and ask if they've received it; if they say it's probably mixed in with the other mail, you can point out that it's the one in the red envelope with the goofy drawing in the corner. It will be noticeable.

The Business Card

It's always a good idea to have a business card ready for anyone who might offer you a booking or has an important connection. If you get involved in the comedy scene (as I advise in the next chapter), you may make important contacts, and phone numbers spontaneously scribbled on a club's napkins or torn-off slips of paper too often get lost and show a lack of professionalism.

A business card can be as elaborate as you want to make it, but the basic, necessary information is your name, what you do (stand-up comic, comedy writer, ventriloquist, impressionist, etc.), and a telephone answering-service

Here are two examples that have come across my desk so many times it's impossible for me to ignore them. They both made it into this book, which proves the theory about keeping your promotional material individualized and in constant use. Ventriloquist Ken Groves has a logo (left) that tells you immediately what he does and who his two "partners" are. Whatever investment he might have made in hiring an artist to do the drawing, and in the time and effort involved in the whole process, it was well worth it in the long run. Whenever his promotional material goes out, his contacts in the industry don't even need to read his name, credits, or bio anymore. One look tells everyone in the know that it's Ken Groves.

Comedian Joe Lowers has taken the art of the address label to new heights with a couple of goofy photos, a home computer, and the saying, "I'm not your average Joe!!" His anything-for-a-laugh attitude (especially in his "smashed face" look), can entice bookers contacted for the first time to open his package to see what this guy's all about.

number through which you can be contacted. You can also add any extras you'd like, including your logo; a mailing address (I recommend a post office box or an office address. As with phone numbers, be careful with how much home information you give out); the city where you're based; a fax number; an e-mail address; a website, if you have the means to put one on the Internet; even a line from your act that gives the best example of who you are.

A good printer can help you set up your business card, while your humor, business sense, and creativity can make it distinct from everyone else's. The following are two simple examples of working business cards:

A Few Cautions

Those are only a couple ideas of how to take standard practices and use them to make yourself noticed from the rest of the crowd. Use your imagination and you'll come up with many more during the course of your career.

At the same time, remain professional. Remember that you are in a business and that showing others respect is good common sense. Consider the following.

If you've had no prior contact with someone who can hire you, special-delivery mail can create the impression of an overbearing personality, and gifts could be perceived as a bribe. Little promotional gimmicks such as pens and fake Rolex watches can be cute, but most people in the entertainment industry (regardless of the age-old reputation) don't want to feel they can be bought or swayed by such ploys.

And, of course, you shouldn't go in the opposite direction and send your promo C.O.D. (Cash on Delivery—not to be confused with the show *Comics on Delivery*), even if they've asked you to send it. If you do, you'll most likely be the one stuck with a returned red envelope with a goofy picture in the corner!

> *"The first time someone across campus yelled, 'Hey, Carrot Top!' I thought, 'Oh Lord, do I really wanna do this to myself?!'"*
>
> CARROT TOP

Can You Relate?

Let's say you have the chance to contact someone who can help with your comedy career. Can you relate to any of these statements?

• Your pictures don't look like you.

• You don't have a résumé or bio.

• You don't have a video.

• You have a video, but the picture is shaky and fuzzy.

• You have a video, but your act is inaudible because of a bad sound system or audience noise.

• You have a video, but it's an hour long and your best material is surrounded by a lot of jokes that don't work.

• You're waiting to meet with someone who has more power within the industry.

• You've made other plans for your career.

If you identify yourself in any of these statements, you need to engage in further preparation. Once again, these indicate the telltale feeling that you haven't adequately prepared to make a serious go at a professional comedy career.

To better get this idea across, take the two most important words from the above paragraph, "preparation" and "professional," flip them around, and put them together. If you're still clueless, I'll do it for you: *Professional preparation*. That's the whole key to becoming a working comic. Be professional and be prepared. As always, I happen to have a little story to demonstrate the idea. . . .

One day in Los Angeles, I received a frantic phone call from a very good comedian friend of mine who had learned that a famous movie director was searching for him to audition for a role in a future film. This comedian didn't have a service number, any promotional material to speak of, or a current videotape. He had always been well-respected enough to get bookings with just a phone call or by contacts through his regular performances at various New York City comedy clubs. These contacts were the only channel by which he'd heard the director was looking for him. A frustrated assistant had started calling the clubs and another comic had relayed the message to him.

When he called, he was desperate for a videotape of himself and thought I might have access to a television spot he had done earlier in the year. Unfortunately, I didn't, but I told him how he might go about finding it.

As my friend scrambled to put something together as a submission for the film role, the director, who was on a different schedule, had put the word out that he was searching for a comedian–actor.

Others who also fit the part's description had their material ready and on its way to his office before my pal even had the chance to dial the phone number I had given him.

Needless to say, he's still struggling for his big break while another comedian added a major credit to his résumé, picked up a fat paycheck, and gained a little bit more recognition with bookers looking for a name act. If you want to put a title on the lesson to be learned, try "Professional Preparation."

Reaching the Right People

Being involved and knowing what's going on in the comedy world means meeting and staying in touch with the "right" people. The "right" people are the ones who can help your career. Now, don't get snobby, because that could include just about anyone. An audience member might give you a good premise for a joke, or a club's assistant manager may know someone who could help you find work. You'll never find that out if you're not involved.

In fact, next to building up stage time, being involved in the comedy industry is the most important recommendation I can make to anyone serious about a career in stand-up. You must get a feel for what the business is all about. You can read all the books you want, but there is no better way to gain knowledge than through real-life experience.

It's the same as with anything else in life. If you want to be an accountant, you learn from someone who knows accounting. If you want to swim, you get in a pool. Comedy is no different. You want to know people within the comedy scene. Ideally, you want to meet those who are successful, ambitious, positive, and knowledge-able enough to give you constructive advice or criticism. If you hang out with poor performers, it's possible you'll wind up like them. Not that the opposite is true, but success sometimes has a way of rubbing off.

I've witnessed too many people talking about how successful they're going to be without actually making an attempt to make it come true. Actually, a lot of people talk a good game, but you learn much more about it from the ones who are playing.

Your best way of contacting the "right" people is by going to the comedy clubs and meeting the performers, managers, and club owners. You have an interest in what they are doing, so ask their advice. People will feel flattered.

Approach a comedian after his or her show and say how much you enjoyed it. Tell the club owner or manager how much you like the club. Ask about audition nights. Be friendly, and never overbearing. Let them see your face and hear your name a few times so you're recognizable.

Your Initial Involvement

Start locally. If you're starting at the amateur level, try to be a regular performer or visitor. If a local club has an open mike every Tuesday, be there *every* Tuesday. Even if they only allow a certain number of performers each night and you must skip a few weeks between sets, go anyway. It will show you're interested and want to be involved. It's also a good way to make yourself more familiar to the people running the show. You'll learn a lot just from being there, and you might even be asked to perform if they happen to have an open slot or extra time at the end of the night. That won't happen if they are unaware you're a comic.

> *"The club owners are the people who deal with the different agencies. They set up different showcases. You have to be on their good side to be on that list."*
>
> *REGGIE McFADDEN*

Of course, to get involved in this way you must continue writing new material. As people see you more and more, they get to know your act as well as you. You want to perfect the material you have, especially if it's working, and attempt something new—a new joke, a new premise. Practice working off the crowd, even if it's just for a minute.

Working on something new not only gives you a goal for each performance, but also lets everyone know you're working to improve. It keeps your act fresh and gives you a reputation for diligence and ambition.

Once you're involved and have that reputation, people can't help but notice you—so be prepared. It's always a good idea to have your business card ready for an important spur-of-the-moment contact in a club.

After you have made contact with people, the best way to keep in touch with them will be to keep working and send postcards. When you work, it gives you something to write about on the back of your postcard. A simple "Hi" will do occasionally, but if you mention you're working, it sometimes increases your demand. This, too, shows you're serious about your career. (I'll explain fully how to use your promotional materials in the section on booking yourself on the road.)

That gives you an idea of how to make contacts on a local scene. If you are in an area with a few different clubs, you can do the same in each. You'll meet people who have experience and you'll probably learn something from them. When you're ready to expand your horizons, you should find both their knowledge and acquaintance helpful.

Developing Personal References

Personal references can cut through a lot of the red tape you'll encounter in pursuing your stand-up career. One phone call from a respected comedian, booker, agent, or manager can usually get you in the door faster than an unauthorized mailing. So another reason it's so important to be involved in the comedy world is to cultivate personal references.

If you land a booking on a show with another comedian who is a regular performer at another club you'd like to play or who has access to a contact you'd like to meet, ask him or her to put in a recommendation for you. Make sure that comic likes your act first! It never hurts to have a good recommendation from someone who's already been hired by the person you want to work for. You can then follow with a phone call and take it from there.

> *"We can walk out there with nothing prepared and definitely get into a routine. . . . Invariably, audience attention will discover our jokes for us."*
>
> TOMMY SMOTHERS

Booking Yourself on the Road

When I say "working on the road," I do not include showcase clubs. The owners of showcase clubs (such as the Improv), where industry professionals hunt for new talent, are doing you a favor by letting you perform where you can be seen. (Even headliners with national television credits are rarely given more than twenty minutes to perform their sets in a showcase club.) You may end up with only your cab fare and a meal, but you will have come out ahead.

Working on the road is a *job*—it's employment. If you're a professional comic, it's how you put food on the table and money in the bank. When I first started in the field of booking comedians, I used to tell them how lucky they were to travel the globe without having to dress up like the guy in the Navy recruiting ads ("See the world . . ."). Acts used to call my office from Alaska in the summer and Florida in the winter, and I'd tell them what a great life they must have. That was in the beginning, before I started getting calls from Alaska in the winter and Florida during hurricanes. Then I learned the real story.

I realized that many comics talk about game shows and soap operas because that's what they spend their days watching while living in hotel rooms thousands of miles away from their families. One town blends into another, and I've witnessed more than a few comics asking where they are before they go onstage to talk about the local scene. It's a hard road—and it's one that most aspiring comedians must travel.

As with any job, working on the road is what you make of it. Compare yourself to a traveling salesman (no jokes, please). Your goal is to travel from place to place, sell your product, and get paid for it. The difference is, you are the product. Actually, you may have it easier than the typical traveling sales "rep." While he or she must go from door to door showing the product, you can accomplish some of the preliminary footwork from the comfort of your home. Your business partners are your press package, telephone, fax machine, e-mail, and local post office. Even though rejection is common to both professions, you can focus in on only those who might wish to hire your services.

> *"The headliner liked me and suggested I call this club where he was playing next. I did, and they hired me, so I drove up there and did a week. That's how it started."*
>
> TOM RHODES

A good way to get work on the road is to be a regular performer in a club that is part of a *network*. The local Sammy's House of Yuks may not have a branch at Caesar's Palace in Las Vegas, but they might have a few other rooms in which they book acts. Get yourself established at one and inquire about how you might be able to play the others.

If, just getting on your feet, you don't have an agent or manager, or if there are no clubs near you with connections to supply you with more work, then you must take charge, be aggressive, and chart your own path. (A good agent or manager would book you in various clubs and provide you with enough work to support yourself; I'll discuss how to find and work with a manager or agent in the following section.) For now, I assume you've got a survival job, a rich spouse, or some source of income to rely on until the bookings come through. You'll need it. Also I assume that by now you have a good video of your act, a headshot, a résumé, and bio.

I assume you have stage experience that you have used to develop a good act. I won't even mention how, if you accept a job before you're ready, you run the risk of experiencing one of the worst feelings you can have onstage: being pulled off by management in an effort to calm a dissatisfied audience.

I won't breathe a word of that scenario because your act should now have been tested enough in front of open-mike crowds and in local performances for you to know what response you'll get. You're confident you can stand onstage and entertain an audience for *at least* twenty minutes—*right?*.

> *"I would go to L.A. and work a little bit, and I would go to New York and work a little bit. I used to have arguments in New York because people would say, 'If you were here every night, you could get discovered.' But I chose to be on the road and make a good living for a decade where nobody knew my name."*
>
> JEFF FOXWORTHY

Remember, twenty minutes is just a guideline. On the road, whether it's with written material or an ability to work off the crowd, you will normally be expected to have twenty minutes or more as an opening or middle act. Headline comics do an hour or more, but you're more likely to be struck by lightning than to get top billing for your first shows. Headliners are booked through agents, by reputation, and on the basis of their credits or past performances at the club.

Many club managers are only concerned that the opening acts make the proper announcements (drink specials, discount nights, coming attractions, etc.), along with giving the audience a few warm-up laughs. But you may be asked to "stretch" your time for various unexpected reasons. This could include the next act not arriving on time or (surprise!) the audience indicating they want you to continue. Naturally, you don't want to be signaled to stretch and then stammer and sweat because you have no more act, so *be prepared* to keep 'em laughing for an additional fifteen minutes.

To book yourself on the road, you must first locate clubs to work in. This can be done through many different sources. One good way to get a listing of comedy venues and of whom to contact is through the various publications available at bookstores (especially with a good theatrical or performing arts section) or at comedy clubs. During the past few years, there have been quite a few comedy magazines, newspapers, and booklets that have come and gone. I'm sure there will always be new versions on the stands. And to stay in business, each should do its best to keep track of club and personnel changes and publish frequent updates.

There are also bookstores that specialize in entertainment publications. New York and Los Angeles have the Drama Book Shop and the Samuel French Bookstore, respectively. Their current phone numbers are easily available from the city's directory service. Call and explain what you are looking for; if they have the necessary information, they'll let you order it for delivery directly to your home.

A good newsstand will also carry various out-of-town newspapers and magazines. Look through their entertainment sections and advertisements for any listings about comedy and comedy clubs. Where there's a show, there's always a phone number for reservations. Call and ask whoever answers how you go about getting a booking.

The Internet can also supply you with many leads if you look through the comedy categories. Gather the important facts such as locations, phone numbers, and names, then call the clubs and ask for information about auditioning.

> *"You've got to do as much stage time and writing as possible. You will be found out, because the cream does in fact rise to the top."*
>
> BOBBY COLLINS

Of course, while gaining your stage experience, you should ask other comics where they play. Find out who books the rooms, what you might expect to find there, and what their reputation is. You should ask:

• How much do they pay?

• Do they pay for travel?

• Do they offer accommodations?

• Are meals included?

• And, most important, do they pay promptly?

Most club owners know that if they want to have quality shows with quality acts, they must be reliable in paying their acts. They cannot refuse to pay or cut salaries after the performances are completed. Still, you hear stories that some try to do these things.

Once you have collected a list of clubs along with their addresses and names of the talent bookers, send them your promotional material—your headshot, résumé, bio, and video. Write a cover letter that introduces you and states your purpose in sending the materials. When writing a cover letter to any given club, remember that it does not need to be a comedy routine. Make it professional and to the point. Keep in mind that it's being said by *you* and communicates why you want to play the club.

The following are a few hints about the basic points that might be included in a cover letter. You probably want to state that:

> *"Anytime you have a gig on the road . . . call a newspaper. What's great about getting press in a newspaper if you're working in a club is that if they like the artwork, they'll run the photo."*
>
> RHONDA SHEAR

- You've heard great things about the club.

- You're interested in performing at the club.

- You have experience and consistently get good audience response.

- You have enclosed a videotape of a recent performance that you hope they will consider when booking their club.

- You appreciate their time and attention.

- You will be calling within the next two weeks to follow up.

If you've been performing regularly in a local club, ask the talent booker there to write a letter of recommendation for you. Better yet, write your own and ask him or her to sign it. You can do the same for any college, corporate, or benefit shows that you add to your credits—if you received a good crowd response and the people in charge liked you. Include copies of the letters of recommendation you get in your promotional package.

Wherever you might play, there will be a local newspaper. Since many have entertainment sections that focus on local events, use them to help your career. Learn from the club what papers are in their area and whether they advertise in any of them. Mail the publication a press release stating who you are, where you're from, some of your career highlights, and when you'll be performing in their area. Follow it up with a phone call and request that they preview or review your show. You may be surprised how many positive responses you get.

As you continue to perform, you could be fortunate in obtaining some flattering newspaper reviews about your act. By all means, include these also with your promotional material.

Those letters of recommendation and positive reviews could help sway a talent booker who might be unsure of your experience. An impressive promotional package should be an announcement that you're a seasoned, professional performer.

To cut your costs, you might want your videotapes returned. If so, enclose a self-addressed envelope in your package with the correct postage affixed. If a club asks to keep your video, always agree to it, because their booker might be searching later for a new act or a last-minute booking. If your tape happens to be the one they find, it could lead to future work.

If you already have shows booked, it's a good idea to inform your contacts of the dates you are not available. This is called an *avails sheet* and is something we'll get to in a few moments. It helps with the club's scheduling, and makes it clear you're in demand.

Now, having done all this, what do you do next? You wait.

If the clubs don't contact you, give them a call in approximately two weeks. Ask if they've received your mailing. If they claim they haven't, or say it's lost in the pile of others, this is where the earlier mention of creativity comes in handy. If, for example, you mailed it in an unusual-colored envelope, then describe what it looks like. It might be right in front of them!

Ask when would be a convenient time for you to call back. Make a note of it and follow through. Never act too impatient or important to be kept waiting. 'Hold' buttons are very popular on entertainment-industry telephones, and are used often to tame someone's attitude problems. So be pleasant and let them set the tone for the conversation. (It should be personable or professional.)

Don't be shy or afraid to call. Comedy is a business, and offices are equipped with business phones. If you reach these offices at a busy moment and get grumpily brushed off, call back another day at a different time. It's usually rare when someone is a sourpuss twenty-four hours a day.

While you do not want to be overbearing or a pain in the you-know-what, you do want to be aggressive on your own behalf. Be assured, if you aren't, others will be promoting themselves boldly. They may not get the job, but often their tape will be viewed, even if it's only to get the performer out of the talent booker's hair.

After ending the conversation, send your contact one of your postcards. Whether it's thanking him or her for a job, for the time spent speaking with you, or to say that you're beginning to work on a better tape or that you'll be calling back at such-and-such a time, send a postcard.

I cannot emphasize enough how important postcards are. Too many acts don't realize this and rely only on their videotape and an occasional phone call. You've got to keep your name and face in the booker's mind, and a postcard is the easiest way.

At this point let's say that within roughly two weeks you've gotten your promotional package and a postcard across that person's desk, and placed a personal phone call, too. Wait a week, or until the booker's "best time," and call again. Inquire about your tape. If the person still hasn't seen it, send another postcard and call again in another two weeks. Continue this until he or she watches it.

Once the booker has seen your tape, ask about possible bookings. If he or she liked it and wants to book you, schedule it.

If anyone sounds unsure about your work, you should offer to perform at the club as a showcase act, provided that this can be done conveniently for both of you. In other words, continue selling yourself.

If a booker simply is not interested, ask for his or her expert advice about your act, and ask if you can submit a new tape in the future. Whatever the case, follow with a postcard and use that method to stay in touch.

Another important method to help bookers make their decisions is to regularly send your updated avails sheet. This is a copy of your performance calendar listing when you are (and are not) available for bookings. I usually recommend sending these once a month, or when there are any changes in your schedule. (Two sample avails sheets are shown on pages 72 and 73.)

As with every promotional tool, avails can be made different and original. But they should *always* be easy to read and use. You might want to list only the dates you are available, or include additionally where you are already booked so the person you are mailing avails to can route you easily into his or her club.

After you get a booking, try to make the most of your visit to that location. Send your avails, and call other clubs that are along your route and try to schedule additional performances. Make it clear that you are already a working comic and are looking for performances during the neighboring weeks. In other words, try to schedule a mini-tour to make the most of your time on the road.

One last caution, however: Avoid calling a club that might be a competitor to the one you've booked in the same city or town. That's the best way to not get invited back to either!

RON LAUGHSTER
(555) 555-5555

COMEDY SCHEDULE (YEAR)

JANUARY
1– 3 / AVAILABLE
4–/ Harrisburg, PA (afternoon)
4–/ Harrisburg, PA (evening)
5–14 / AVAILABLE
15–19 / Cincinnati, OH
20–26 / Cleveland, OH
27–30 / AVAILABLE
31–/ Youngstown, OH

FEBRUARY
1–/ Youngstown, OH
2–/ AVAILABLE
3– 7 / New York, NY
8–12 / AVAILABLE
13–16 / Newark, NJ
17–23 / N/A
24–28 / Philadelphia, PA

MARCH
1– 3 / Evansville, IN
4– 9 / Cleveland, OH
10–12 / AVAILABLE
13–15 / Detroit, MI
16–17 / AVAILABLE
18–23 / Chicago, IL
24–29 / Gary, IN
30–/ Toledo, OH
31–/ AVAILABLE

APRIL
1– 6 / Saginaw, MI
7–10 / AVAILABLE
11–13 / Flint, MI
14 / Ann Arbor, MI
15–/ Kalamazoo, MI
16–/ AVAILABLE
17–/ Toledo, OH
18–20 / AVAILABLE
21–25 / Nashville, TN
26–30 / AVAILABLE

MAY
1– 5 / AVAILABLE
6–11 / Pittsburgh, PA
12–13 / Erie, PA
14–27 / AVAILABLE
28–30 / Wheeling, WV
31–/ AVAILABLE

JUNE
1– 4 / Columbus, OH
5–30 / AVAILABLE

JULY
AVAILABLE

AUGUST
1– 4 / New Orleans, LA
5–/ AVAILABLE
6–10 / Baton Rouge, LA
11–30 / AVAILABLE
31–/ Erie, PA

SEPTEMBER
1–23 / AVAILABLE
24–26 / New York, NY
27–30 / AVAILABLE

OCTOBER
1–15 / AVAILABLE
16–/ South Bend, IN
17–20 / Evansville, IN
21–29 / AVAILABLE
31–/ Cleveland, OH

NOVEMBER
1– 5 / Cleveland, OH
6–30 / AVAILABLE

DECEMBER
1–23 / AVAILABLE
24–28 / NOT AVAILABLE
29–31 / Toledo, OH

GRETA GAB

St. Louis, MO
Phone (555) 555–5555
Fax (555) 555–5555

(DATE RANGE)

June	4	Harrisburg, PA	**October**	6–11	Pittsburgh, PA
	15–19	Cincinnati, OH		12–13	Erie, PA
	21–26	Cleveland, OH		28–30	Wheeling, WV
July	1	Youngstown, OH	**November**	1–4	Columbus, OH
	3–7	New York, NY			
	13–16	Newark, NJ	**December**	AVAILABLE	
	24–28	Philadelphia, PA			
			January	1–4	New Orleans, LA
August	1–3	Evansville, IN		6–10	Baton Rouge, LA
	4–9	Cleveland, OH		31	Erie, PA
	13–15	Detroit, MI			
	18–23	Chicago, IL	**February**	24–26	New York, NY
	24–29	Gary, IN			
	30	Toledo, OH	**March**	AVAILABLE	
September	1–6	Saginaw, MI	**April**	16	South Bend, IN
	11–13	Flint, MI		17–20	Evansville, IN
	14	Ann Arbor, MI			
	15	Kalamazoo, MI	**May**	1–5	Cleveland, OH
	17	Toledo, OH			
	21–25	Nashville, TN			

The first sample Avails Sheet lists the entire upcoming calendar for comedian Ron Laughster. Month by month and date by date, it tells you where he will be and when he's available to perform. A booker with a specific date in mind can look up the month and see if Ron's schedule is open. He can also see when the comedian will be in his or her area and add shows to Ron's travel route.

The second Avails Sheet for Greta Gab gives the same information. She lists only the dates that are already scheduled, leaving the rest for bookers to fill in. As with all other promotional material, both acts have their name and phone number listed at the top so the avails sheet can be used as a separate and easy-access reference for making contact with them.

What About Managers and Agents?

Managers and agents are a major behind-the-scenes part of an entertainer's career. They are in business to obtain work for, and further the careers of, the performers they represent.

The idea behind having a manager and/or agent is to make the business aspects of performing easier and more prosperous for the talent. Their jobs vary according to what they offer and what you need. Managers and agents could take care of everything from your bookings and travel arrangements to your onstage image and making sure you pay your credit card bills on time. They might even suggest or be a sounding board for what type of comedy material is best for you. Whether it's a big agency, small agency, personal manager, or business manager, they should do whatever else it takes to move your career to continually higher levels.

> *"I made an error with my first manager because I should have gone with someone a little bit smaller. That agency was a mega-house; it was like a factory. . . ."*
>
> REGGIE McFADDEN

The reasons managers and agents get into this business are as varied as they are for the performers. Some may enjoy the excitement involved in entertainment industry, while others may thrive on the deal-making possibilities behind different projects. There's also the chance that a little of the spotlight will shine on them when their clients are in demand and finding major popularity.

Whatever their reasons may be, the incentive behind this business is simple. The more money the talent makes, the more money the manager or agent makes. I don't mean for that to be a greedy statement; being a manager or an agent can be a difficult job, and the income from a job is the reason why people throughout the world go to work. To put it in comedian terms: A good reason to work hard is that the amount paid a headliner is a lot more than what an opening act normally makes.

Ideally, once you have a manager or agent (we'll take up getting one later), all you should have to do is write fresh material, perform it, and keep improving your act, because you're paying him or her to do the rest. A manager usually takes about 15 percent of your earnings while an agent gets 10 percent. Those figures can go up or down depending on the representation, type of performance you do, or how the booking was secured. If you take those general figures together, that's a quarter of your income.

Let's say you're willing to do the extra work in order to save 25 percent of your income. I'll admit, it is a lot to give up. What managers and agents do should make them not only affordable but necessary. Managers and agents make their living networking in the entertainment industry. You, as a performer, do networking, too. The difference comes when you look at what it means to be successful: When you've risen above the average competition and can make a living at performing, your *major* concern is working on your act.

In the early stages of a stand-up career, gaining stage experience while maintaining an income from either an outside job or working on the road doesn't leave much time to do the necessary behind-the-scenes projects that can further your career. With a manager/agent, you can concentrate on creative work while he or she handles the career moves.

Still considering doing it alone? You can and should in the beginning. Everything I've explained in the preceding chapters about how to get onstage, gain experience, write an act that works, create promotional materials, and make the basic contacts to establish your career is for you to do yourself. If, as a result, you're now working regularly in local clubs and on the road, then you're headed for the day when you'll feel you should be getting better billings and more money. You may miss out on certain auditions because you're stuck for a week in another city—an example of a time when good representation would make a difference.

Even after you've established your career, you can personally call bookers and attempt to convince them you're ready to headline or should be offered a separate audition, but you're most likely to be one among many who are doing the same. A good talent representative's job is to have lines of communication available and to handle these important tasks so you can concentrate on performing.

If proper representation can raise your income and status in the industry, then it's worth the price and affordable. Here's a simple example. Say you're at the level where bookers know they can schedule you for $200 a night. You need the money and have to work regularly to pay your bills. This leaves neither a lot of time to do showcases for better employment nor leverage to negotiate for more money. The solution is better jobs and a higher income. A lesser workload, say at $500 a night, allows more time for industry showcases, which can lead to higher income and a higher profile, which, in turn, can lead to a more successful career.

The Manager

The manager is a independent contractor who is contracted to work for your benefit. A manager's duties can vary from state to state, depending on professional licensing requirements and laws. For instance, in California, a manager is not allowed to promise paying jobs for clients. This is the agent's lawful right. Even though some managers do make such promises, it usually comes back to haunt a manager if a client wishes to terminate his or her services. The client need only prove that the manager booked him or her into a paying performance and that it's a violation of the contract. Case dismissed —manager fired with no further commissions due. (It's always wise to check the state's codes before signing a contract.)

Different managers are better at different duties, but the manager's main duty is to "shape," or "mold," the performer into a true professional and into a product (sorry about that term, but your creative abilities are for sale) that employers will want. Some may see a raw talent and recommend their own creative ideas on how to shape that talent into a successful package. They may suggest a different look or even a different verbal delivery of the act to make it better for television or clubs.

> *"Managers . . . don't feel I give up enough to let them do what they do. . . . I have been hands-on in my own career for a long time. I want to know what's going on."*
>
> RHONDA SHEAR

The Beatles provide a good example of a manager's creative presentation of an act in a way that improved their status and income. The Beatles' manager, Brian Epstein, saw the group during one of their frequent local club performances. They had the right sound, but their stage mannerisms and dress were not professional enough for the mainstream public at that time. It's a well-known story of how he put them in suits, and stopped them from swearing and eating on stage. He knew enough not to change their music, but put together a professional package that helped to open the doors of the conservative early-1960s recording industry. After their phenomenal success, they were free to express themselves in any manner of dress or speech they wished. The lesson to be learned is that their manager helped shape their image and worked hard at furthering their career. And while they were unburdened of those tasks, they concentrated on their music.

Managers can have many other duties besides tending your image or recommending the contents of your act and its presentation. They can collect your fees and pay you, handle your publicity, select the photographers and pictures you use, coordinate your travel, and find you a good agent. Always remember that different managers do different things.

Before ever signing a contract, discuss with a prospective manager what he or she can offer and what you expect. Managers usually will not enter into a short-term contract if they can expect to reap none of the benefits after they have worked hard to get performers to a successful point in their careers.

Do your best to make sure you'll have a good working relationship. Do you like that person and do you feel he or she likes you? Do you trust that person? What is his or her reputation with other comedians, clubs, and talent bookers? Do you both agree on the direction your career is about to take? What is this person offering you and what are you offering in return? Together, what do you see as long-range goals for you?

The Manager in Action

You're sitting in a club. The lights dim for the evening's entertainment and anticipation stirs the crowd, a voice announces from the sound system the identity of the comedy club's master of ceremonies. Meanwhile, a shadowy figure slips into the room. The brightness of the spotlight on a lone performer walking onstage starkly contrasts the darkness where the audience sits. As your eyes adjust to the dim light in the back of the room, you notice that the shadowy guest has blended in with the surroundings.

Other lone figures enter and gather at unoccupied tables. A nod or handshake is the only demonstration that a bond between them might exist. Noticeably bored by stock jokes or tired premises, they maintain a low profile that keeps them from fitting in with the evening's paying customers. Like spies working behind enemy lines, they make mental notes of the performing comics and, if a favorable judgment is rendered, they'll request a meeting, pass a business card, or offer a next-day phone call. If the judgment is negative, no contact will be attempted. This clandestine operation is a process that can be repeated whenever, and wherever, unknown talent may be found.

What you've observed is an average working night of a talent manager searching for comedy's next big star. Skilled, with the traits of a chameleon, he or she might change dramatically according to the situation. The manager can become the very visible and unofficial host to anyone in the room who can give his or her client employment. If the interest is already high, the manager can play hard-to-get until the offers meet a desired target. Other evenings are spent alone in front of a VCR working through mountains of videotapes submitted by unrepresented acts, while most daylight hours are spent working the telephone in search of a client's next big break.

A Visit to a Management Company

Management companies are similar to performers: They come in all sizes, excel in different areas, and can be grouped according to their credits. Usually, the older and larger ones represent a greater number of established acts. Smaller companies may choose to work with only a select number of clients while keeping their careers on a more personal-interest level. The newer ones might have the freshness and energy of people out to make a name for themselves in a competitive business.

We'll look at one management company, Messina/Baker Entertainment, which seems to balance all of the above qualities, through the work of one of their highly experienced managers, Dave Rath. Owned and operated by partners Rick Messina and Richard Baker, the Los Angeles-based company handles the careers of some of Hollywood's biggest comedy stars. Still, they work hard at maintaining the personal touch and aggressiveness of the smaller and newer kid on the block. Their clients include Tim Allen, Drew Carey, Janeane Garofalo, and many young, up-and-coming actors, writers, and stand-up comedians.

As a talent manager at Messina/Baker, Dave Rath is known for being aggressive and involved. He keeps his finger on the pulse of Hollywood's comedy industry by maintaining business contacts in person or on countless phone conversations and by frequent visits to showcase clubs—he was one of those "spies" in the back of the darkened club.

I asked Rath how he got involved in the business side of comedy. "I just fell into comedy. I walked into the Improv one night with a friend to see a show. I thought it might be a good place to get a part-time job as a doorman, just to kill some time and make some money. Budd Friedman hired me on the spot, and a month later I was at the Santa Monica club as the showroom manager. After about six months I got recommended for a talent coordinator job on the HA! Network, which was the first comedy channel."

Rath came to know a number of comics and people in the business and went on to work for Fox, MTV, and Comedy Central. At the same time, he started a management business, which he eventually merged with Messina/Baker. I asked Rath to explain what a manager actually does.

"It really depends," he answered. "For me, it's always about the talent. There are a lot of managers who do a lot of different things. I'm part babysitter and therapist, as well as a manager, which is someone who gives advice to someone on a career. One thing I try not to do is make the decisions. It's a question of gathering information, being on top of it, and then helping your clients make decisions as opposed to answering for them.

*Manager Dave Rath.
(Photo courtesy of
Susan Maljan)*

"It's also a question of identifying young talent and being able to discuss with them what *their* objectives are, and then educating them along the way as to what their options are. We're not really driven to encourage people just to make deals, just to make money; it's really a question of developing as an artist. For some, that means staying where they are—say, in San Francisco—to develop as an artist. When there's a *reason* to move to Los Angeles or New York for work, that's when to do it. They shouldn't just go there to get into the mix.

"Become the best writer, the best stand-up you can be, and then when you're ready, it'll start happening. You'll start showcasing and getting material out and getting feedback. That's when you'll attract a manager or an agent. The idea is to really develop on your own. Then things will become available.

"With a lot of our clients, we encourage them to do stand-up, to write, to act, and as something develops and there's interest in one area of their talent, then that's where they'll have to focus," he said.

"After the talent has developed and is ready to work, does Messina/Baker (and other management companies) focus on finding their client a good agent?" I asked.

"Not necessarily," he answered. "Actually, Tim Allen and Drew Carey, two of our top clients, don't even have agents. We perform a lot of the functions of agents because our relationships with studios, networks, and people in the business are as good as an agent's. But a lot of our newer talent are not stand-ups. They're more actor- or writer-driven, and the theatrical and writer clients really do need agents. Someone needs to be plugging away for them."

"The thing I'm learning now is that young talent don't necessarily need management right away," he said. "You need a manager when there's something to manage—when you get a deal or a show and you have to start making those kinds of decisions. What we do with young talent is guide them and help them along the way. We might be one, two, or three years away from making any money with them, but because of the success of some of our profile clients we're able to do that."

"Since you're in California," I noted, "you can't work as an agent without a license."

"In California and most states, like New York, agents have to be licensed," he answered. "Managers, legally, aren't supposed to negotiate or solicit work.

"There are a lot of misconceptions among young people, especially with their first manager. They pressure them to get them work, and it's hard for a manager to say to some of them, 'Well, you know what? We're not supposed to get you work, and we're not supposed to negotiate. You're supposed to do that on your own.' And they say: 'Then what the hell do I need you for?' So, for young talent, stand-ups especially, and with our relationships in the business, we're able to get them work. But when the actual contracts come in, at that point agents or lawyers are brought in to negotiate and to finalize the deal. We don't do the negotiating."

I asked him about the contracts the firm signs with clients and got a surprising answer: "We don't sign anybody," he revealed. "Some management companies do, but we don't sign papers. We like the idea of not having to force people to sign a contract, because management is so personal. Rick Messina and I, especially, take it so personally that we're good friends with our clients. It's more of a family approach that we have, and we find it works best for us."

I mentioned that I had spoken with comedians at all different career levels who claim they would be doing better if they only had a good manager. I wondered what advice he would give those who were looking for representation.

"If you're a stand-up, become a great stand-up," he advised. "Again, stay in your city and become the best one there. Then, when there's a reason to go to Los Angeles or New York, go and showcase. Talk with managers and agents.

"The best way to select representation is to really identify your own needs. What kind of person are you? Are you the kind of person where you need to talk to your manager every single day about your girlfriend and a lot of other stuff? Or do you want somebody that is just out there working for you? It really depends on your own personality. Some people don't need managers. Some just want a good agent who can hustle for them, and they handle their own lives—and save some money that way.

"But, for the most part, when it gets really busy, you need that 'filter.' You need someone to handle the phone calls and requests. You need someone to bounce ideas off of and help you make decisions. That's what I really think the most important thing about a manager is."

Which is better—for the talent to pursue a manager or wait until a manager approaches him or her?

"Again," he answered, "it depends on personality. I don't usually respond that well to people who solicit me. I'd rather find somebody and meet and talk with him or her. One thing I've learned is that the more people sell themselves, the less there is to them. I think people should be really confident in themselves. If they go out and do what they do, they will be discovered. If they're writing and they're doing well, they will be approached, as opposed to going out and making those contacts.

"I sometimes sense resentment from stand-ups that I haven't chosen to work with or haven't booked. It's nothing personal, but when people put you in the position of having to evaluate them, they'd better be prepared to be rejected. Sometimes it can be a very difficult thing."

As with the talent it manages, the company has continued to grow in different areas; its managers can explore other areas of the business as a result of the success of certain clients. "We try to stay focused on management, but sometimes it's difficult because there's a lot of production opportunities that come up, too," Rath said. A good manager knows opportunities are out there and available, if he or she only takes the time to look.

I asked Dave Rath one more question before his disappearance into the darkness of another comedy club. "Do you enjoy what you're doing?"

"I love it," he confessed. "I can't even believe I'm getting paid to represent someone like Janeane Garofalo, who, to me, represents integrity and talent to the fullest. Also clients like Tim Allen and Drew Carey, who are so incredibly talented. Plus they're human beings too. That's something I'm really glad about. In my position now, the most important thing is that I get to work with people that are good people, not just talented. They're easy to work with. I don't have to put up with head cases anymore, which is really nice."

The Agent

The full term for this person should be "booking agent," because that is what his or her job is: An agent books your performances.

Like managers, agents may handle their jobs differently. Some may only concentrate on booking their clients into live club or theater performances. Others may be television, commercial, literary, or film agents. Some may do it all. Your job, or your manager's, is to find the best agent for you.

Basically, an agent works to secure paid employment for his or her clients. Your agent should have the contacts to book you where your level demands; if you're a middle-level act or a headliner, the agent should know where and how to book you as such, and if you're ready for television, whether you're performing or writing, the same is true.

An agent will negotiate your fees and performance requirements—in other words, how much you get for a certain number of shows. There are many different methods an agent can use to do this; performers need not attempt to know what they all are, but ideally, the agent finds a demand or a need for you and works out the best possible deal for your appearance. For more profit at a lower travel cost, the agent may base the booking on the availability of other shows in the area. He or she may also book you and other clients piggy-back style, getting the booker to agree to use another of the agent's acts to secure the desired booking. This can occur when one client is in great demand. This isn't always considered ethical, but it is done.

Remember that an agent, like a manager, is a independent contractor who is contracted to work for your benefit. A good business relationship, characterized by understanding and trust, is extremely important to minimize any disagreements that might occur concerning the direction of your career. You may not always agree with the agent's ideas, but you should be secure in knowing he or she is on your side.

A Visit with an Agent

The Roger Paul Agency is located in Manhattan's theater district, in an area called Hell's Kitchen. Small when compared to some of the industry giants such as the William Morris Agency, agency head Roger Paul competes in the same market by booking his clients for personal appearances and building their careers.

Similar to performers who discovered early on their desire to go onstage, Paul chose his future profession when he began managing local rock bands while in high school. He continued his management activities while attending the University of Miami; eventually he started booking most of the entertainment for the school. He went on to book talent for Variety Artists, in Minneapolis, and then headed back to the South to work with a Florida-based booking agency. Next, in New York City, he learned video production, got more involved with music, and joined a small college agency that booked concerts. That was followed by a stint at Spotlight Entertainment, in Manhattan.

"I went to this small showcase club," Paul recollected, "and told the owner, 'Let's do something better. You've got a big room, over 300 seats, let's do the bigger action!' This big Italian guy said, 'Ya ain't gonna sell anything.' I brought in a comedian and told him we'd give him $300 versus a percentage of the door, whichever is greater. He walked out with $3,000 for one night. A Wednesday night! After that I started my own agency."

Paul can be found in comedy clubs around the country supporting his clients, looking for new talent, and keeping an eye on the world of entertainment generally. One night I cornered him and got an insider's view of life as a talent agent.

"The difference between a manager and an agent is the following," he told me: "A manager is responsible for shaping artists' careers, preparing their presentations, working with them, marketing them and, generally, doing things to advance their career. Agents are responsible for employment. They're the ones who put the bread and butter on the table. They don't get the credit in the business, but they're the ones who are really responsible for moving an act and keeping it going.

"My job as an agent is to find employment for these guys, whether they're middle acts or headliners, and I have to go all around the country to do it. It's not just limited to comedy clubs. It could be theaters, concert halls, stadiums, casinos in Las Vegas, Atlantic City, or on Indian reservations. It could be cruise ships. I may book my clients as opening acts for concerts, or as the concerts themselves. I'll also do packaging—that is, put different acts together to go on tour.

"It's also my responsibility to get the artist moving in the right direction with the career. We've got to work closely with the manager, getting the right publicity and making sure it's updated. The manager always has to make sure the press kits are put together."

I asked, "Do you need a license to be an agent in New York or Los Angeles?"

"Yes," he replied. "In New York, you can sort of get away with being a manager and an agent, but in Los Angeles, you cannot—it's illegal. You have to be one or the other. You can book shows in different states, but since my office is in New York I need a license there."

I asked Paul about the agent's commision. "Some agents take up to 15 percent," he replied, "and some managers take up to 20 percent on corporate events or big deals. I like to do a sliding scale. I take 10 percent. But then, after I make an artist $100,000, I take 15 percent. I don't think artists are going to be too mad with that little less money. They'll be quite happy because it's something for both parties."

I told him that many comics want to know if they really need a manager if they can find an agent that will work with them.

"It depends on where you are in your career," he observed. "If you're really doing great, you need a manager to make sure things are running properly with your schedule. Your agent will be too busy booking the dates you're getting. A manager can also act as a publicist as well. But the reality today is that a lot of artists are just using agents. The agents are getting them a lot of work *and* advising them on their careers."

He agreed that having a manager makes it easier to get a good agent. Some comedians work as hard at finding an agent or manager as they do on their comedy material. I wanted to know what was the best way for an agent to discover somebody new.

"Word of mouth," he said quickly. "What people are hearing and what people are saying. Basically, we can't always be out there all the time, so we have other people be our ears and eyes. A lot of times our friends call and tell us about acts. Everybody tells everybody about certain people. That's how I hear—people saying 'Hey, this comic is good. . . .' Recommendations help.

"It doesn't matter where they're from either, because I've also found acts from videotapes," he stated. "You want to send good-quality tapes, because we don't want to watch it while squinting our eyes or turning our VCR way up so we can hear it. And, if you're going to send us tapes, you've got to catch us right away, within the first few minutes. If you have something that catches us, we'll put you on. If not, we lose interest, and you're gone. It's not always fair, but this is business; we've got to make money and can't really take the time. That's especially true for the big agencies; they can't take the time to decipher all those tapes. I average about ten tapes per week. I'm going to be looking at five tapes tonight. I always ask for ten minutes or less so I can just get an idea of the person and whether it's worth it. If it's worth it, I'll get a longer tape.

"If I do like someone's tape," he continued, "I want to see him or her do a set. I want to talk with the person. I take it to the next step, set up an audition, depending where the act is from, and see how it goes.

"Remember," he advised the young comic, "Persistence pays in this business—persistence, more than aggressiveness. If you're persistent with someone, just checking in every so often with a phone call, you're going to get your break. If you're too aggressive, you're going to turn people off. They don't want you in their face, because everyone else is in their face. Agents, especially, have their own clients.

"That's how I got my own agency going. I was persistent. So many times I've called clubs and asked, 'Hey, you got a fallout?'—meaning a cancellation? And they've given me one shot. I send the right person in and *boom*, they give me another chance, then another, and it builds."

"What's the best part of your job?" I asked him.

"You mean besides the money," he laughed, "which isn't great at times? The thrill I have when I can get my client a television show for the first time, or a gig a young comic wanted so bad—I remember when one of my clients got his first *An Evening at The Improv,* and I could hear him crying on the phone with happiness. Wow, what a great feeling. It's amazing when you can do that for somebody."

Of course, I had to ask, "What's the worst part?"

"Everybody hounds you," he lamented. "The abuse. Everybody! It's the truth when it's said there are a lot of ups and downs in this business. But I love what I do. I eat, sleep, and breathe this. I'm married to it."

Finding a Manager or Agent

Just as when you deal with contacts to book yourself on the road, use your promotional package and personal references when you're looking for a manager or an agent. If you don't live in the same city where they are located, you'll have to depend on your videotape as an introduction to your act, which is another reason why you should make it the best you possibly can.

Agents and managers, like other members of the working force, occasionally move to different offices, jump to a competitor's team, leave the business, or strike out on their own. It's a large, important part of the industry, and the frequent changes can make it difficult to keep track of someone you may have been contacting for representation. There are various publications that list agencies and management companies. These are often updated and are available by mail order or from theatrical bookstores.

You'll also be surprised at how quickly news of personnel changes moves through the "comedy grapevine." Stay active in the clubs and keep up with your personal promotion, and you'll probably learn the information before anyone has a chance to type it up, send it to a publisher, and get it to the bookstores.

Finding an agent or manager can sometimes depend on where you're located. New York and Los Angeles are both known for being centers of the entertainment industry, and there's always a good chance that you'll be seen just by performing regularly in the clubs. Remember, you never know who might be sitting in the audience while you're onstage.

Agents and managers in both these cities have the opportunity to see a lot of comedians in an assortment of different clubs. It's a highly competitive business, because their jobs can depend on finding the best new talent on the scene. They have the opportunity to watch acts over and over and determine if the comedians have the ability and talent to be special. They can also tell if an act has gotten stale or if there is no real promise beyond what a comic is currently doing.

Comedians based in both New York and Los Angeles also have an advantage in learning firsthand which agents or managers might be best for their careers. They can observe them on a fairly regular basis and see what acts they represent. Are those acts successful? Are their careers headed in the same direction you feel yours should be going? Which agents or managers might already be interested in you? Which ones do you want to be interested in you?

New York and Los Angeles comedians might have the convenience of approaching the agents and managers and personally handing them a video and/or a promotional package at a comedy club. The comedians can report on where and when they're performing and ask these professionals to watch their act. They definitely find opportunities for more person-to-person contact and the chance to be seen.

But don't start packing your bags while deciding which coast to move to. That's not something I would ever recommend unless you've already had it locked in your mind that you'd like to be a resident of either locale. There are plenty of agencies and management companies all over the map that have enough bookings available to keep funny comedians busy.

You can mail your promotional packages and videos to whichever ones you choose, and follow up with phone calls and postcards exactly as we discussed earlier in dealing with comedy club bookers. In fact, many of these managers and agents are the people scheduling shows for these venues. If they like your tape, be persistent; you could eventually get a booking at one of their clubs. If you're in an area where they're located, they might be interested enough to come out to see you. If not, they'll get reports from club owners who will usually make it very clear whether you were good for business or not. Continue to generate good reports and they may eventually approach you about handling your career. That's when you decide if they're right for you.

Beginning comics should not even concern themselves with agents or managers at their early stage of the game. You can find enough work and continue to improve with the methods we've discussed earlier. Opening acts don't need representation—just determination, dedication, and an awareness of how this business is run. When the time comes that good representation will help take you to the next level, you'll know it.

In Performance

Presenting . . . You!

Each time you walk onstage, consider it the reward for all the hard work involved in attaining that moment. It's your opportunity to entertain, display your talent, wit, and humor, make your points, right the wrongs that might have held you back in the past, and, most importantly, get laughs from an audience. This is truly the place where there are no rules (a quick nod to certain club, theater, and television policies, thank you!). Be yourself, be someone else, or be something no one's ever seen before. Your performance is where all your previous efforts have taken you and, ultimately, where your future in the comedy industry begins.

Each performer is an individual, and should be treated that way. There is no "set" way to stand, proper clothes to wear, or areas of the room that you should, or should not, work toward. Ideally, the spotlight and the attention are on you and you're there to take advantage of it.

What you, as the comedian, have to ask yourself is, "What is it about *you* that makes you comfortable and best conveys what you are trying to say?" I've heard plenty of horror stories about club owners or managers, comedy coaches, other comedians, and so-called good friends telling new comics exactly what they should be doing onstage and when. They've actually directed the act, as they would an actor in a play, and shaped it into what *they* think is best for the newcomer's comedy presentation. Honestly, you wouldn't believe some of the comments I've heard sitting through various "advice" sessions that have taken place in clubs, diners, cars, living rooms and everywhere else an "expert" has been given the chance to speak. Sources (who shall remain nameless to protect their dubious reputations) of these nuggets have come out with these examples:

"You should never sit down. This is 'stand-up' comedy." (Yeah? Try telling that to Bill Cosby.)

"Don't do pratfalls or slapstick. It makes a comic look too silly." (Are you listening, Jim Carrey and Michael Richards?)

"Center yourself at the middle of the stage and don't pace around. You'll keep the audience's attention better." (Do you think Robin Williams and Steven Wright would agree?)

"You should wear a hat. You'll look funnier with a hat." (That one really threw me at the time, and still does. The unfortunate comic who drew that remark probably didn't even own a hat at the time, but spent the next few weeks going for more than a few different looks before taking his act to another club.)

You'll probably hear a lot of different comments on your road to discovering who you are onstage, but stay true to yourself. Listen to what is said, but don't take it as gospel. Mull it over in your mind to decide whether it's helpful advice or pure nonsense. Don't let others stifle what you want to do. Their taste in entertainment most likely doesn't match yours, and you'll discover what is best for you, and the audience, through your experiences onstage.

> *"That's what I'm trying to do. Something a little different. My hero is George Carlin, but people like him do just the opposite of what I do. . . ."*
>
> CARROT TOP

Now that I've said all that, don't shut yourself off completely from agreeable "helpful hints." As I mentioned before, there are managers and agents who are in the business to help mold their clients into employable acts. Once they know more about you, they can suggest stage clothing, techniques, and a delivery style that is already based on where your material and stage persona have taken you. This is something that is a personal decision between an artist and his or her representation. It should be talked through and experimented with thoroughly onstage with the results decided by audience reactions.

Still, I know new comedians want advice on stage techniques, and I've been known to give it, especially in my workshops, where there are many who might be working on a stage with a microphone, spotlights, and an audience for the very first time. What I tell them are not things that I have made up. They're comments I've learned from people in the industry whom I respect and happen to agree with. They're very simple, but can make a difference in how you're perceived by experienced bookers looking for experienced talent.

If you take the microphone out of the stand and hold it, don't just leave the stand in front of you, but move it away—perhaps to the back of the stage, or where you can lean against it or use it as part of your act . . . whatever. Just don't leave it positioned all naked in front of you while you're standing behind it talking. More than one talent booker sitting with me in the back of a club has uttered the word "amateur" when that situation has occurred.

Remember that you're not a Las Vegas "lounge" singer, an image that long ago became a parody for comics (think of Bill Murray's fabulous routines on *Saturday Night Live*). Holding the microphone cord in your free hand and whipping it around or rolling it up, letting it go, and rolling it up again can be very distracting. People will be more interested in watching what you do with the cord than in what you are saying.

As far as "stage presence" goes, some comedians may be told they have more of this quality than others. The term can mean a lot of different things. I've commented to acts with big, happy smiles and an obvious excitement over what they are doing that they have a great stage presence. I've also said it to others who seemed grumpy and hunched over with the weight of the world on their shoulders. It's really about how you sell your act to an audience.

The fact of the matter is, when you're standing solo onstage in a spotlight before an audience, you already have a stage presence. Whether you're outgoing or shy, grounded or constantly moving, loud or soft-spoken, doesn't matter. It's all about feeling comfortable and having confidence in what you are doing. As you continue to perform and improve your act, you may realize in front of a laughing audience that you are emitting a real stage presence.

"Energy" is another important term for new comics to remember. Don't misunderstand and think I'm talking about jogging around the stage or having to manically shove your delivery down an audience's collective throat. That may be what your act is all about, but for many it's not. Energy comes when you are interested in what you are talking about; it's the opposite of "uninterested." There are some wonderful comedians who act and sound bored about everything around them, but they are conveying this to audiences because that is what's interesting to them. It almost seems as if they want to get these thoughts off their chests and out of their minds, but that, in itself, gives them energy.

Never stand on a stage and think, "Well, this next joke is really no good, so I'm just going to say it and keep going." If you can mentally convince yourself that someone might be interested in the humor (why would you have put it into your act if you never thought it was funny?), then you will deliver it with some kind of energy. As I've said before, try never to waste your valuable stage time or that of an audience that has come out to laugh.

As with any other tips and advice from the "no rules" comedy arena, these suggestions are merely that: suggestions. I've found they have helped new comics gain onstage confidence that they would eventually have learned anyway through experience. You'll develop your own stage techniques as you continue, and probably come up with a few personal dos and don'ts that will enhance your individual performances.

Improv to Improve

All of us at one time or another have given ourselves a mental beating with the thought, "I should've said . . . !" Whether it would have been a witty comeback, a stunning insult, or a wry comment aimed at a certain situation, your brilliant mind *could have* snuffed out an insurrection or proved you were in complete control if only you'd said . . . !

Sound familiar? Sound like a recurring event? What if it happens to you onstage?

Welcome to the world of improvisation and (gulp!) hecklers, each of which is proof that there is no "fourth wall" or television screen between a live working comic and the audience.

> ## "I've been doing this so long that I've seen and heard just about everything, and I'm pretty much ready to handle anything that goes on with an audience. Nothing's new."
>
> — JEFF DUNHAM

Improvisation is the skill of making something up "on the spot." In comedy, it's the delivering of an ad-lib, or impromptu, punchline. It's a flexing of your mental muscles and coming out with something that you probably hadn't thought of before or, at least, said onstage. It's a valuable technique to use to get the audience involved in your show, a way to find new comedy material, or to handle wiseguys in the audience.

Many comedians make a habit of talking to their audiences and learning a little information about a few. We've all heard the standard comedy club questionnaires, "What's your name? Where're you from? What do you do for a living?" They're not exactly unique icebreakers anymore, but they tend to get a conversation going.

The fun results from the answers. Once you open the door, you never know what an audience is going to bring in. A good improviser can, seemingly, pull laughs right out of the air, but unless you're gifted with a quick mind (and even if you are), it's a smart practice to keep those mental muscles tuned up. Who knows, you might accidentally fall into a whole new comedy bit, or (and I'm gasping again), get yourself out of a jam with a heckler.

Handling Hecklers

A heckler is anyone who tries to interrupt a show, either verbally or with physical antics aimed at the performer. Hecklers want to draw attention to themselves. Loud, drunk, annoying, and ignorant might be some typical definitions of a heckler from many comedians. But some acts relish the opportunity to blast someone who dares to match wits with a professional.

Depending on the comic, a heckler either disrupts the flow of the performance or creates the chance for added laughs. Either way, a good comic is always prepared, because sooner or later, it's going to happen.

One of the questions asked earliest and most often in my workshops is how to handle hecklers. What do you do when someone yells out something, anything, aimed at you and the rest of the audience hears it? You never know what's going to happen and when, but you'd better believe that after it does all eyes will be on you for a response. What do you say?

There is no set answer for that question. A quick wit and comfort in what you're doing, which comes from plenty of stage experience, are your best resources. But if you suffer from the agony of our earlier statement, "I should've said. . . ," then I suggest you get some training.

The best way to do this is through a class in improvisation. Practice that bolsters thinking on your feet, and doing it fast, is an invaluable experience for anyone interested in making a living onstage. Different improv classes teach different methods, and books have already been written describing their various techniques. But there's nothing that can match the actual lessons learned by doing it. Games and exercises are used to get your thought processes in high gear, which is what you need, and want, when you're on a comedy stage.

Everyone seems to know all the better stock lines, which is a good reason to advise against using them. A stock line is a comeback or joke that has been used in dealing with hecklers in the past—and appears to have been around forever. Unless you're coming up with an original comeback, you run the risk of more than a few audience members having already heard it:

"Hey! I don't go to your job and tell you how to flip burgers!"

It was funny the first time you heard it, remember? The second time it might have been okay. The third time? Well, you get the picture.

Like anything else in comedy, the more original you are the better chance you have of succeeding. Be aware of what's going on around you. Acknowledge something when it happens; you'll look pretty foolish if everyone else notices something and you're the only one ignoring the situation. Play off it and have as much fun with it as you can.

If a heckler is *too* distracting, a good club will normally take care of the situation and either quiet down the rowdy person or escort him or her out. But, then, how many good clubs are there, really? I've heard lots of tales from road-working comics who have been onstage and forced to deal with the situation alone. They do what they can to quiet the heckler, get the laughs, do their time, and hope the distraction doesn't ruin the show.

If it's clear that the disturbance will ruin the show, the person onstage should ask the club's management or staff for assistance. If they care about their business, they'll realize other customers are there for a comedy show, not a free-for-all.

The best advice I've heard is *never* give the microphone to a heckler. Don't fall into the trap of thinking you'll allow the person to look like a fool while attempting to do what you've worked hard at doing onstage. You'll only give a jerk more power and volume, and with no guarantee that you'll get it back. Either handle the situation or get help.

Two Masters of Improvisation

When playing off an audience, there are two comics who rarely leave the room thinking, "I should've said. . . ." More often than not, they've said it. To Scott LaRose and Rick Overton, improvisation is comedy. It's also writing, acting, and a solid base for their careers. They practice the art of quick thinking and reacting to whatever situation is thrown at them and eagerly look forward to the nightly challenges.

As solo stand-up comics and actors, they've each appeared in countless television shows, commercials, films, and comedy clubs. LaRose remains one of the most recognizable faces in commercials and sitcoms; Overton's credits include an Emmy as a writer for Dennis Miller. While not a comedy team, some of their most enjoyable moments are when one joins the other on stage for impromptu performances where improvisation makes for a memorable show.

For both LaRose and Overton, improvisational skill is not some gimmick locked in the back of their minds and used only for occasional laughs or put-downs. They've trained and developed their techniques and are having too much fun to keep them hidden.

"Improvisation is one of the fundamental beginning tools of comedy that will guide you from the point you start from to every-thing else you do," offered Overton during a two-on-one con-versation, with me being the loner.

"It gives you the true feeling of power," added LaRose, "to know that at any point and at any situa-tion you can improvise your way out of it. And Rick, what are the rules of improvisation?"

Comedian Scott LaRose.

"To listen. . . ," began Overton.

"Right! Correct!" yelled LaRose.

"To move the scene forward," Overton continued, undeterred by his pal's cheerleading. "Never deny what the other person runs into the scene and gives you." He paused to think of the third rule. "Actually, they all rhyme: It's never deny, always reply, and never ask why.

"Always asking 'why' just slows it down. 'Why do you say that?' 'Why do you want me to go on a boat?' 'Why do you . . . ?'"

"I've learned so much watching Rick," LaRose said. "The day that I got to improvise with him for the first time, I said, 'Oh, man, finally I'm doing it with the right person.' Because

Comedian Rick Overton. (Photo courtesy of Susan Maljan)

you could be out on the biggest limb and he'd be right there for you."

"Well," answered Overton, reacting to the unexpected, "right back at you, man!"

"Oh, c'mon, man!" shot back LaRose.

Finally sensing a breach in the action, I jumped in with a question about training. LaRose said, "I was at New York University in the theater program, where they had an improv teacher named Omar Shapli. He was a famous Second City guy. I had an improv class two hours a day, five days a week. It was the most amazing thing in my life! This was the first time I could go into a class and lie all day long! I can *lie!* And they loved it; they want you to lie as much as you can and create that reality as much as you can. And have fun with it."

"And yet, be honest about your lying!" added Overton.

"Exactly, because that's truly what acting is, I think," said LaRose. "When you see someone acting and it looks like it's happening for the first time, you know it's not, because it's acting. In improv, it is happening for the first time. Lying honestly is a good way of looking at it."

"It helps you," said Overton, grabbing the moment. "It really helps you. You can get out of some corners you've painted yourself into—that otherwise you probably couldn't get out of—when you have improv tools."

I wondered how easy it was for them to carry their improv techniques into stand-up acts. How do you improv when you're up there all alone?

"Actually play the moment," improvised LaRose, "which is, again, what acting is. Truly living in that moment and not worrying about falling. Just knowing, in that moment, you're going to be able to get out of it.

"When I improvised in New York," he continued, "I actually started my act with no stand-up material. Remember the old game, the old 'fill in the blank'? I did it as a detective: 'It was 3:15. I got up and I went to the kitchen to make some soup, and I got a _____.' Then the audience would fill in the blank. That's how I started my act; I'd do twenty minutes of improvising. And it started to come slowly by playing with audiences, that's how the material came, and it still does come that way."

Both have prepared material they can count on, but they're not poster boys for the disciplined, stay-at-home-and-write-for-eight-hours-a-day style of comedian. They have their bits, but they excel in the dangerous waters of making it up as they go along. Overton confided, "You know, there are *keepers*—that is, while you're going along you think, 'Oh, that's good! I can use that again.' You've got to refine it, hone it, and fine-tune it, but you've got a new bit."

"I definitely don't sit by the computer and write eight hours a day," admitted LaRose. "I have plenty of notepads, but it's usually just the idea or the topic jotted down. From there you wing it, you throw your attitude in with it. And all of a sudden, before you know it, it turns into a beautiful bit. And after about ten years you'll have a good forty minutes of material."

"Ten years. . . ," mulled Overton, joining his friend in laughter. "That's like the Zen Master, you know? 'You are not ready for the test joke!'"

Jumping on their laughs, I said, "I've seen you both onstage plenty of times and you both seem fearless. Were you always like that? Were there any problems just winging it?"

"Well," answered Overton, "in the very beginning, I felt a little better having a lot of my material memorized from stuff I wrote down."

"I was always fearless," laughed LaRose. "I never cared about having jokes. I was just so happy being onstage and playing and, again, living in that moment and making stuff up."

They talked about the technique of "making stuff up" and keeping it rolling.

"You act out the scene a little bit," Overton said. "You put some different characters in it, and you take them on a conceptual ride."

"Yeah!" continued LaRose, "You see comics a lot of times get offstage and you think, 'That was such a great joke! But if you'd *kept going* with that—there was so much more! You haven't even touched it. You were not even close yet.'"

"Those comics," said Overton, "for their style, that was it. That was the whole joke. But for us, that joke was just the beginning of a whole bit. They don't realize that that thirty-five seconds could've been twenty minutes."

On behalf of comedians just starting out, I asked: "When you go onstage individually, do you have something in your head already, like an outline? Or now do you just go up there and whatever comes out, comes out?"

They explained that there are "two modes" of working: "There's some stuff in there that's kind of pre-set," said Overton.

"Right!" added LaRose. "There's two ways. There's one where I just want to have fun and, truly, just go up and improvise for a good twenty-five minutes. But there are times where I think, 'I've got to do six minutes with a beginning, middle, and an end, and get off. Make it clean and crisp.' That's when industry people are there. It's kind of sad in a way, because you want people to be able to see that side of you where they say, 'Wow, look at Overton doing all that stuff!'

"And yet, you know what they do with that? They say, 'What are we gonna do with all that stuff?' So that's why you've got to rein it in sometimes and just say, 'Okay, I won't do that much. I'll just do this part.'"

Being seen as fitting into an industry category "is often what it's all about," Overton pointed out. "And then they'll say, 'Well, you're not the tool-belt kind of guy. . . . And you're not the guy with the big box of toys. What guy are you? We don't know what guy you are, therefore, we don't know where to place you.'

"We defend our style. We're kind of proud that they're not so quick to categorize us."

"Right! Even in acting," continued LaRose. "To bring improvising into acting, most of the time it pisses off the writers. But when you throw stuff out there, when you improvise with a good script, you can't get a better performance than that. You get the most believable 'in the moment' stuff you've ever seen. But it does piss off a lot of people when we go into audition and I toss out, 'Here's the way I see it. . . .'

"We get that reputation for being a loose cannon," he said as they both started laughing hard again. "But I couldn't go to each thing and do it exactly the same way every time. It would bore me."

Knowing these guys could follow me in a different direction, I asked about what to say to hecklers: "There are a lot of 'stock lines' out there. Do you have any in your back pockets that you can pull out?"

"I don't go down to McDonald's and show you how to flip burgers," said Overton.

"If I want any shit out of you," joined in LaRose, "I'll squeeze your head."

"But using a stock line in those situations is setting yourself up to get slammed," voiced LaRose. "Again, if you're not working in the moment, truly, with that person, no matter who it is. . . . Like the time—it was in Idaho—I walked on, for literally two seconds, and didn't even get a chance to say hello! I went to the microphone and some lady says, 'Oh great. Another tall Jew-boy.' Now, what do you do with that? When I haven't said a word and she doesn't even know who I am? How the heck does she know I'm Jewish? LaRose is not even a Jewish name, but I am Jewish. I just said, 'I'm sorry, but'—and the whole place went silent—I said, 'How much did you pay to get in here?' And this is just going with the situation, but not immediately. I knew I was gonna trash her, but you have to build to that; you can't just go right to it. So she said, 'Three dollars.' And I said, 'Well, it's only five dollars to get in here. I guess you got two dollars off because it's Nazi Night.'

"The place went nuts! They threw her out within seconds.

"And that's not a stock line, Nazi Night, but it could be," LaRose went on. "It's playing the situation the way it is and being comfortable that you're taking a few beats there, that you may not be coming right back with the zinger, you know? Let the mind think it up for a second and then work it out. You'll come up with something."

"Use the information that is given to you in the circumstance," added Overton. "The crowd will appreciate that you did."

"It'll look twice as good," advised LaRose.

"I once had a time," recalled Overton, "when a woman, maybe in her late fifties, with gigantic hair, was sitting with these two guys. And they're all just sauced. 'Blah, blah, blah'—kinda loud, you know? Dreadful people. And they're talking right down in front. I said, 'Excuse me, ma'am. I don't know which one of those guys is your husband. . . .'"

"And she reaches for the guy on her right and says, 'He's my honey.' And I said, 'Well, that explains the beehive.'"

"That was great!" laughed LaRose. "Beautiful!"

"They'll always give you something if you're watching closely enough," said Overton. "They'll dump information on you. You know the way they say the criminals always want to get caught by the amount of clues they leave? These people want to get busted, and if you've got your scanner on, you read it immediately. You pull two or three phrases out and twist and tie them back into something, and you just dump them back down their throat."

"That's a good way of looking at it," added LaRose. "Hecklers are just like psychotics. They want to get yelled at."

"You know the way the crowd laughs derisively at the heckler?" asked Overton. "He'll start laughing and clapping too, like it happened to someone else! These people always come up after the show and say, 'Man, you got me good. You know, I was helping you out.'"

"Right. Yeah," LaRose groaned with sarcasm. "Wasn't that helpful? Thank you very much."

As they both broke into hysterics, I wondered if this could be the beginning of a future bit, or if there was a chance I could become a punchline. I improvised a heartfelt goodbye as they broke into a series of puns, and almost felt sorry for the next comedy club patron who says the wrong thing at the wrong time in front of LaRose or Overton.

When Industry People Are Watching

Even my two favorite improvisers, above, had to throw in an exception concerning their wild onstage world for the times when industry people are in the audience looking for talent to fill specific jobs. Again, I'll use the term "showcase" for this, but the definition is somewhat different from that of our earlier discussion about booking yourself into comedy clubs.

An *industry showcase* is one set up by casting directors, television talent coordinators, comedy festivals, agencies, and management companies. They happen on a frequent basis in Los Angeles and New York (especially when television networks are casting roles for sitcom pilots), but can also occur in other major cities when there is a nationwide talent search for a specific person to fill a role. I've spoken with industry people who travel the country in an attempt to be the first to discover new performers. Friends call friends who might have a friend in casting and talk about acts they've seen in their hometowns.

Industry showcases normally consist of many acts appearing for a short time onstage—anywhere from three to seven minutes each. The talent scouts attending can usually make a decision in only a few minutes—and they usually do—on whether a given comedian is who they are looking for. The benefits of seeing acts this way works for both sides. Industry people can see a lot of talent without digging through a pile of videos or driving to various clubs hoping to catch the right performer. They can also see how each comic compares with the competition, what makes him or her unique, and how much an audience enjoys that comic.

The comics who make up the list of performers on the showcase get an audition. They get to show their stuff in front of a live audience and have a chance to prepare beforehand instead of being surprised at the last minute over who is in attendance. They can also avoid much of the frustration of trying to entice someone from the industry into going to a certain club at a certain time to see only them. The comics who are involved get the chance to show off their best work in an environment where they have been making their reputations, the comedy club.

But with such a short time to make an impression, you can't afford any moments that might not display your work in its best light. The idea is to do the material that best defines you and your act or that suits the role that you are being seen for. The best way to do this is to put together your "greatest hits," as a musical artist does for an album. Use material that you know works and can be counted on from previous performances in front of laughing audiences. As Scott LaRose said, "There are times where I think, 'I've got to do six minutes with a beginning, middle, and an end, and get off. Make it clean and crisp.' That's when industry people are there."

One thing you can expect if you perform in an industry showcase in New York or Hollywood—where many of the clubs are called showcase clubs—is that a large part of the audience is there for a specific reason. There can even be showcases for one industry person, such as the owner of a club where you'd like to perform. And while the rest of the audience will hardly notice, that person may leave after a given performance. There will be times the club has seats reserved for several industry people amid the audience. If the show starts at 8 P.M., but the showcase doesn't begin until 9 P.M., many of these invited guests won't arrive until just before the later hour. Then, once the showcase is over, most will usually get up and leave, no matter who's on next. It could be a national headliner, but their job is done and that's why they were there in the first place. This puts a big hole in the audience and makes the performing spot that follows one of the toughest of the evening.

Industry showcases can sometimes be a pressure-filled event for less experienced comedians, and just "another day at the office" for those who have been through the process before. As with anything else that's important to you in your career, you want to make the best impression you possibly can. But try not to sweat it out too much. I've never heard of anyone "bombing" at a showcase and never getting another opportunity from someone else. Relax, enjoy yourself, and look at it as another step on the ladder of learning about the comedy industry. Once you're onstage during a showcase and performing, your experience of the many different audiences you've entertained will take over. After that, it's out of your control. If they like you, great. If they don't, maybe the next visitors will. Keep working and be ready for every opportunity. As I've said before: You never know when or where you will be seen, never know who might be sitting in the audience, so always make an effort to give your best performance.

Expanding Your Horizons

Why are some of the hottest people in television and films coming from the stand-up community? Watch closely and you'll probably witness it every night: In sitcoms, dramas, movies, and theater, stand-ups are being employed and stretching their talents far beyond comedy club stages as actors and writers.

Good comedians are good performers. They're funny and have the talent, experience, and ability to entertain an audience. Otherwise, they wouldn't be considered good at what they do. Whether they are high-energy, low-energy, doing characters, or just being themselves, good comedians will be noticed and in demand. They also have a good chance of being hired as actors or writers in the television and film industry. Stand-up comedy is one of the best ways an entertainer can showcase his or her talents. It's an up-to-the-minute example of one's creativity in front of an audience that has paid to be entertained.

Casting directors and producers, forever on the lookout for new or established talent, frequently visit comedy clubs. The clubs showcase performers' abilities and creative ideas, and more often than not a good comedian will put on display a character or comic personality that he or she has already fully developed through extensive stage experience. Writers creating a sitcom with a comedian as the central character have more than a blank page to start out with, if they already know the comic's onstage persona. In fact, the entire idea for a program can be based on the comedian's act. Onstage, Tim Allen was already the "man about the house" before *Home Improvement,* and Jerry Seinfeld wondered about the absurdities of Manhattan before *Seinfeld.* The show *Grace Under Fire* was already being developed before the producers saw Brett Butler, but once she was signed, the role of Grace took on many of the characteristics she was using in her act. It's just less work for the creative team to form a show around a developed character than from scratch. This is the case when shows are looking to cast interesting supporting roles also.

Don't Expect Miracles

How are the comics who go into TV and film getting hired?

They are being seen, period. Like any good salesperson, you must get the product viewed or demonstrated in front of the

> *"The Tonight Show producer was in the club's restaurant, and they brought him into the showroom to see me. The truth is, the waitresses at the Improv got me on the show!"*
>
> DOM IRRERA

potential buyer. This can be done in many different ways, some more acceptable than others.

We've all heard stories of celebrities who were discovered when they least expected it. Telling jokes while working behind a deli counter and doing magic tricks instead of mixing drinks behind a bar are two cases I've heard of "being in the right place at the right time"—of luck and talent crossing paths. But such miracles mainly happen in old show-biz movies, in which a major talent executive points to an unknown and shouts, "Put that kid in the picture!"

A lot of success can be attributed to "who you know," it's true. But with comedy the *talent* must be there. The streets of Hollywood are loaded with people who can read cue cards or memorize lines and shoot a dozen takes in front of a camera before getting it right. But comedy takes talent and experience to make it work. Making an audience laugh has been described as one of the hardest things to do in the entertainment industry. Your rich uncle can own as many comedy clubs as he wants and it still won't help your career unless you can make his audiences laugh. That's why it's so important to develop your talent and gain experience, in case you do meet the right person or find yourself in a situation where you can further your career.

If you have the talent and experience but can't get seen by the right people, then you must find a way to make it happen. Don't expect to be discovered sitting at a local lunch counter; realize that real life is different from old show-biz movies.

The Showcase "Audition"

As we've seen, a comedy showcase is actually an audition. It's where you give it your best shot and hope those in the position to give you work are enjoying it and want to hire you. Showcases are low-paying or unpaid bookings that take place on every level of the comedy scene. Whatever the next step in your career is to be, whether it's to be booked at your local club or star in your own network sitcom, someone will want to see you perform first. And the most common way to be seen by industry professionals is through a showcase appearance that slots you into an evening in a club. The casting directors or producers who call a comedy club and arrange to see acts that are right for a certain job might have their own list of people, or they might call agents and managers they know for a list of their clients. Or they might ask the club booker to suggest which performers they should see. Having connected with the club, established a good performance reputation, and used your promotional material effectively could be vital to your being on that list.

A showcase booking can be for any length of time. For a casting director working on a television spot, three to five minutes of your act is sufficient to get an idea of who you are and what you do. The people watching (or judging, which is a term many comics hate) should have the skill necessary to spot new talent. They know what they are looking for and can tell very quickly if you have it. Of course, club bookers will probably want to see you perform longer to guarantee you have enough time to entertain their audiences.

The idea behind a showcase is to offer your best. Don't waste any time onstage, because you probably have little of it. I recommend you only include material that has worked well in front of live audiences—that is, don't try anything that hasn't been tested before. You will learn through stage experience that something you think is very funny doesn't necessarily make an audience laugh. You have no true way of knowing until you test it onstage. An audience will always let you know what works and what doesn't.

If there are other acts showcasing with you, observe what they are doing and try to maintain your originality. You don't want to repeat what they've already done unless there is a premise that's important to your act and you're confident you do it better; or a theme or topic has been requested for that particular showcase. For example: You are participating in an evening for which you are told that the developers of a political show have requested the showcasing only of acts who do political material. In other words, if there are ten to twenty people performing for the showcase (not unheard of in Los Angeles when television networks are scouting talent), don't waste your valuable time repeating what others have already said.

Imagine you are watching the show and the first ten comics walk onstage and say, "Let's have a hand for tonight's host!" You definitely don't want to be the eleventh one to do it. Industry professionals and audience members will soon get very bored with the same beginning. Remember, people looking for talent are normally looking for originality.

Showcases have a life of their own. It's definitely not "just another night" in a comedy club for those involved. The industry professionals are doing their jobs by searching for new talent while comedians are looking to further their careers. Be professional and always ready to perform at your scheduled time. Acts who miss a showcase often find it's much harder to gain a second opportunity, especially with all the competition working to be seen.

One bit of advice: Find out if there's a certain topic the industry folks are interested in. I once scheduled a showcase for *The Today Show* during an election month, and they were only looking for comedians with political material. What they got was something in the neighborhood of fifteen comics each doing five minutes of material about politics. In this case they videotaped the showcase, took it back to their offices, and made a decision that resulted in one of the performers appearing on the program.

One factor that might be out of your control is a search for a certain type. It could be black, white, fat, thin, male, female, young, old—if there's a certain description for a role they are looking to fill, then that's the type of comedian who will be asked to showcase.

Shows that are looking only for new or unknown comedians will be open to all types. What gets these performers an invitation could be their video submission or a recommendation from the club booker or another comedian. When I worked with *A&E's An Evening at The Improv,* I would schedule a showcase for myself to look at new comics every Monday night at the Improv in Los Angeles. During one half-hour I could see six comedians do four minutes each (with the remaining time used by the MC for introductions) and decide if any should be booked immediately for the show, or if I needed to see more from someone at a later date, or none of the above. Sometimes other talent coordinators from different shows would join me in the back of the room and the comedians auditioning had the chance to be seen for a variety of jobs.

Try not to put too much pressure on yourself when showcasing. A case of nerves can almost always be detected. Relax. I know, it's easier said than done, but understand that showcasing is quite common in the entertainment industry. It's important, but if you're good there will be others. Experience, which leads to confidence, is the best way to prepare for a showcase.

Remember your first day at a job? You were probably nervous.

> *"Be there for those showcases. Carry a tape of your act, slip it to the guy who's auditioning everybody"*
>
> REGGIE MCFADDEN

After a while though, your nervousness went away and that job (if you kept it long enough), became second nature to you. It's the same with performing. Get that experience and you'll have the confidence to do well during any showcase.

A Showcase on Tape

Let's go back a minute to your video. Think of it as a showcase on tape, a modern way to do business and a good way to be seen if you live in an area where industry people do not circulate. The idea is to have a tape that best represents your act, the same as a showcase would, and can be mailed or given to film or television professionals when you want to pursue a showcase or an audition before them. This is common practice and a very important part of furthering your career.

Getting Television Exposure

Television is probably the most powerful tool in the entertainment world. The only acts I've ever met who claimed they didn't want to appear on television were the ones who couldn't get on. It plays a major part in status, recognition and, yes, earnings.

Television can work for you, or against you, in many different ways. At its most extreme, it can make or break a career in one night. It's been written that a candidate's televised image during a Presidential debate has done more to determine an election than a grinding schedule of personal appearances and hand-shaking. The same holds true for entertainers. For actors, a TV movie can do more to make an unknown talent recognizable than a career's worth of dinner-theater engagements.

Let's put this into comedian's terms: One appearance on *The Tonight Show with Jay Leno, The Late Show with David Letterman,* or even a local program in a major city can reach more viewers during its broadcast than a countless string of one-nighters across the country. Television, listed as a credit on a comic's résumé, can help to attract better bookings. It indicates a higher level of drawing power with an audience and puts the comic in a good position for asking for more money.

I won't theorize about how television exposure can lead to a starring role in a sitcom or a movie career. Talent, desire, hard work, good representation, and lucky breaks determine that. If those roles are your goal, you first need to be noticed on the tube. Earning your first television appearance can be obtained by several different means:

1. A live showcase audition in a club

2. A good video

3. A good agent or manager

4. A great recommendation

5. A great audition with a casting director (usually obtained by one of the above)

6. The unknown

This is where your hard work has a chance to pay off. Being a part of the comedy scene, you'll naturally become aware of what other comedians are doing, who's auditioning, who's running auditions, and who's making these

> ## *"I wanted to do The Tonight Show. That was the only reason I moved out to Los Angeles in the first place."*
>
> DREW CAREY

auditions work for them. Listen, ask questions, watch television shows that use stand-up comedians, and put together a list of who's in charge of booking talent for these shows.

There are guides available from theatrical bookstores that list casting directors, but quick personnel changes are nothing new in the entertainment industry. These publications can be outdated as soon as they hit the shelves. Since it's good training to watch the shows to learn their formats, watch the credits, and do your best to stay current with who is booking talent.

We've already seen why you should establish yourself at the better comedy clubs in your area. Constantly looking for new talent, industry professionals visit numerous cities and accept recommendations from respected club owners by phone or mail. You want to be on the "A" list of any club that can get you seen for television.

When casting directors for a sitcom or movie call a comedy club and request a block of time to view acts (this happens almost daily in Los Angeles and New York), they'll describe the type of talent they're looking for. If it's for a stand-up comedy routine, they'll ask if there's anyone they should see that they don't already know. The club bookers can almost always add their own recommendations. If you have an agent or manager, getting you on the list of comics the casting people want to see is part of his or her job.

Of course, many situations in show business have been described as a Catch-22, and you may find yourself in the same position when searching for television work. I've heard acts complain often that they can't get a good agent or manager unless they have television credits. I've also heard them say they can't get on television without a good agent or manager.

Well, *you can.* This is where your seven- to ten-minute videotape comes into play. As I said earlier, that's all you need as an introduction for television. The tape should include *only your best material* with little or no "dead air." Plan it as if you were doing a set for *The Tonight Show.* Know what might be censored from network television and eliminate it from your taped set. In other words, present yourself as you think you would be presented on the show. Make it obvious that you're a professional comic.

For the method you should follow for breaking into television, remember how you booked yourself on the road (see Chapter 6). Do your homework, target a show that features stand-up, and send your video to whoever is in charge of casting talent for the show. You may safely assume that the industry professionals connected with it want to discover new talent and watch tapes as well as see live performances. Wait two weeks, and then give them a call. Ask if they've seen your tape and whether you could perform a live showcase for them to see. If they haven't viewed the tape, stay in touch until they do. If they have, you'll very likely get an answer.

I repeat: It *is* possible to get booked on television as a direct result of your video. If it's a great tape with no flaws in the set, it's not outrageous for one of the many cable network shows, for example, to take a chance on you. Anything is possible, but you have to put yourself in the position where it could happen for you. You have to get that tape into the right person's hands.

> *"I would send tapes ...They'd mail them back because I lived in Georgia. My wife kept saying, 'You're not going to know if you could've done* The Tonight Show *unless you go to L.A.'"*
>
> JEFF FOXWORTHY

Consider yourself successful at this stage if you are granted a live showcase. If it's in a different city from where you are, schedule a definite performance date and make arrangements to be there. It's never impossible to reschedule important showcases, especially in the case of an emergency, but for this important date be a total professional and honor your commitment. Just as you remember last-minute cancellations as an inconvenience, so do talent bookers.

Find out how long you will perform during your showcase. Even though a show's broadcast performance might last seven minutes, that doesn't mean you'll be asked to audition for the same length of time. As mentioned earlier, showcases can sometimes be for only three to five minutes, which gives the casting person plenty of time to judge your live performance.

If you don't get a booking or showcase, don't argue about your talent. Ask if you can submit a different tape within three to six months. Then work hard to make it better than the one you'd sent in before. And don't get discouraged. You should know by now that stand-up comedy is a highly competitive business—the chances of failure are better than of success. If you believe in yourself and your talent, stay focused and keep working.

The Importance of Local Programming

Find out what stations are in your area and what they do about programming. No matter where you live, you are part of an entertainment market.

Whether it's in a major city or a rural area, you can be entertained by turning on your television or switching on a radio. Each local broadcast market has its own programming and, usually, network affiliates such as ABC, CBS, NBC, and Fox. Since they cover a lot of territory, don't fool yourself into thinking all the important industry professionals are permanently located only in New York or Los Angeles. Local affiliates of big networks and a given area's independent stations usually have certain hours of their broadcast schedules that they fill themselves. Many programs have started out in local markets and gone national. Now-famous shows by Oprah Winfrey, Phil Donahue, and Merv Griffin serve as examples, as as do two series by improvisational sketch groups: Second City's *SCTV* and *The Kids in the Hall.* Who knows? You might be the next big thing to come out of your hometown market.

The Unpredictable Happens

I listed an "unknown" factor in getting a first shot at television; it's always present in a comedian's career. You never know where or when you might be seen by someone in the entertainment industry. This is why it's important to maintain your professionalism whenever you perform. Never slack off, thinking some audience isn't worth your best effort; someone crucial to your career might be in that audience. People in the entertainment industry move to

> *"If you're a stand-up, stay in your city and become the best one there. Then, when there's a reason to go to Los Angeles or New York, go and showcase."*
>
> DAVE RATH

and from different areas like anyone else. I, for example, am from the Cleveland area but have been employed booking talent in both New York and Los Angeles. I often returned home for holidays and vacations to visit family. Sometimes I went to comedy clubs unannounced, to see comics from the area. How many of them would have done different performances if they had known they had a chance to be on television? As I continue to say: *You never know who might be watching!*

The Comedy Writer's Choice

In almost every comedy workshop I've been involved in, someone has pointed out that he or she was more interested in writing comedy than in performing it. Such people don't have as much desire to be onstage as to write material for other comedians, or for television and film projects.

As with any other career, there are different ways to achieve your goals. Just as bakers have to bake, truck drivers have to drive, and comedians have to get laughs, writers have to write. You must constantly work to improve your craft and make your writing the best you possibly can.

Many of the best writers I've known have come out of the comedy clubs. That's not to say it's the only way comedy writers have found employment—I'm just reporting what I've seen. I always watch the writing credits at the end of televised comedy shows, and I'll admit there are quite a few names I don't recognize. Then again, there are always more than a few whom I've seen perform in a club somewhere. It all comes back to being a part of the comedy network, or comedy scene. It's being known by your peers as having the talent for writing funny material. Some of the comics I've worked with have written great scripts for network sitcoms, or have a number of jokes that would be perfect for a certain comedian. Their dilemma is how to get it into the hands of the right person, and I've discussed strategies at length with various writers who have tried different methods. One of the most popular is to mail a script directly to the production office of the targeted show and hope it is accepted. More often than not, the script is returned unread with a note stating the office cannot accept "unsolicited material." This means that they only consider submissions from an accredited agency or a source other than an "unknown."

Some have actually found a way to get their material directly to a certain comedian through a discovery of his or her mailing address or phone or fax number, or in a chance personal meeting. There are miracles, but put yourself in the position of the comedian. How would you feel if you received unsolicited (there's that word again!) calls at home asking you to try an unknown product? You might listen for a while, and if it seemed to be something you might use, you'd perhaps consider it. If not, you'd simply hang up and wonder why these telemarketers always seem to call during dinner.

Normally, if a comedian is working with writers, those writers are already in place. People who are already familiar are considered for any openings; the job candidate's work is admired and known well enough that the performer trusts the material will work with the stage persona he or she has spent years perfecting.

A popular credit I've seen on many comedy résumés is "writer" for the host of a popular late-night talk show. When I've questioned the comedians about this, they've told me they had been given the use of the show's fax number for submitting jokes. If one was accepted, they were sent a $50 check. The fax number had been referred to them by another comedian or "connection" within the industry. And how did they happen to meet that comedian or get the "connection?" Usually through performing and being involved in the comedy scene.

I've worked with stand-up comedians who make a very good living writing for others. They may write for performers getting ready for a television appearance or as staff writers for a network show. They don't need to go on the road to make a living, and work primarily out of the comfort of their own homes. They aren't stars, but they collect their checks from them, and they do what they've wanted to do: making people laugh.

All comedy writers had to prove their worth somewhere down the line, if not by performing onstage and earning a reputation for comedy writing, then by being in a writer's group (which is a regular gathering of writers who work together while sharing ideas and connections), or through submissions to an agency who believed enough in their written words to submit the material to the "right" places. If performing is not your style, then I suggest you find a copy of *Writer's Market,* or a similar source that lists agents within the entertainment industry. Search for ones that deal with comedy writers. These publications tell you what type and amount of material these contacts wish to receive. Follow these guidelines when you send your material, or call to learn what is necessary for their serious consideration. Some of the listings will be straightforward and state that a reply will come anywhere from two weeks to six months. Others will make it clear that phone calls are not welcome and that they'll contact you only if they're interested.

Following their rules, also be creative and consider some of the suggestions made in the section about booking yourself on the road. If phone calls are not discouraged in your source guide, then call to make a follow-up, just to see if your material has been received.

Postcards, magazine or newspaper articles you've had published, recommendations from working comedians, and anything else that makes you look like a professional writer can and should be used to your advantage. Put together one-page flyers containing your "success information," use your local post office or corner mailbox, and keep your name going across their desks.

One key point to remember: Never put your career on hold and wait for only one particular reply, or stop writing new material until someone contacts you. You're a writer, so continue working at what you do and have new submissions ready in case you get a "bite."

My recommendation on the whole topic? I'm glad you asked. If you've noticed, we've been talking in this book about finding work as a comedian and focusing on performing. As with everything else we've discussed previously, your best bet is to become known within the industry. And what better way to do that than to be in front of people performing?

If you are onstage being funny every night in clubs, someone in the industry is going to take notice. Whether it's another comedian, agent, manager, producer, or anyone else looking for talent, your chances of being seen, heard, and listened to are greater if you're out there doing what you do best. You may not be the dynamic performer who will someday fill theaters and star in your own sitcom, but your talent for writing great comedy will be obvious. How else will anyone see this if they don't have the chance to witness it in front of a live, responding audience? Are you just going to walk up to someone and declare it as a fact that you're funny? Better to prove it.

Writing as a Career Shift

I've spoken with acts that have reached their goals of appearing on *The Tonight Show with Jay Leno* or *The Late Show with David Letterman* who have then questioned what their next career move might be. They've claimed to have no acting talent or desire to go into sitcoms or films, and they've been headlining clubs long enough to know they're ready for something more challenging. Many have turned to writing. Already known by other comedians and industry professionals for their ability, their proven success makes them a desirable member of someone's team.

It is not uncommon in Los Angeles for a few established comedians (whom I would've enjoyed seeing onstage that night) to turn up in the audience to watch a "name" act. On the occasions they were asked if they wanted to perform, they declined because they were "working"—as writers of the material for the comedian onstage.

How did they get the job? Usually through talent, reputation, and contact, by way of the comedy scene, with the performer.

One of my personal favorite stories concerns a birthday party I held for myself at my Los Angeles apartment one year. I put the word out through the comedy network that I was having this gathering, and the turnout was pretty heavy. At one point, a comic I had known for years pointed out to me that a number of people sitting on my balcony were currently nominated for Emmys as writers on *Seinfeld*. It was a very impressive group of stand-up comedians I had known from New York, who were still active performers, but also very skilled and funny writers. They had all made reputations for themselves with a "Manhattan" brand of comedy, and the show's producers were obviously aware that their talents would be right for the show. And since the

> *"You have to develop your art, but you also have to stay abreast of what's going on in the comedy world."*
>
> REGGIE MCFADDEN

creators of *Seinfeld* were also comics who developed their acts in the city, it's doubtful they would have hired writers for that sitcom if they hadn't already proven themselves on New York stages.

The idea is to make yourself seen and heard. There are plenty of opportunities for writers in the entertainment industry, and the lists of shows, specials, and popular new performers are always growing and changing, depending on the public's interest. When something or someone is in demand and appearing frequently on television, there's a tendency to go through a lot of material and always a big effort to find more. Have your writing skills developed and be ready to demonstrate them onstage whenever possible. Remember, somebody will probably be listening.

A Final Note

Now you're ready to experience your own thrill ride through the comedy industry, much of which has been described in the preceding pages. A roller coaster of events might be in store for you, so remember the amusement park warning, "Keep your safety bar locked and your mind in the ride at all times." Okay, so I improvised a bit. But that's what it's all about.

Throughout my experience in the comedy world, I can honestly say I've never been surprised at someone's success, or lack of it. The acts that have made a worthwhile career for themselves were men and women who were "in the trenches" as often as possible. They were innovative and unafraid of failure or success. Not all have become stars, but many are making a good living in this business.

I was fortunate to have the opportunity to watch some of these performers during their developmental stages. It was a fascinating and fun experience to be involved with so many creative talents. Since the best are truly

> ## *"Don't let anyone discourage you. . . . If you really love it, you'll stick with it."*
>
> RHONDA SHEAR

individuals, this book should be considered only an overview of the comedy business. Use it as a basic business outline with experience-backed advice. In Part Two, which follows, you'll read what successful working comics have to say about their profession. Their personal reflections on how they got the job done should help you understand what it might take to achieve success in the comedy industry.

As I've maintained throughout, there are no set rules in the entertainment field, only suggestions and ideas of what has worked in the past. A knowledge of these strategies, applied with your individual creativity, desire, and personal experience, can help to build on your talent for comedy.

"You've got to be working on it constantly or it goes away. And I think people can tell. They'll say, 'He hasn't been working on new stuff.'"

CARROT TOP

But remember, *talent* is the bottom line, and the work of developing it must be done. Don't expect guaranteed success in the entertainment business if you only do the promotional work and don't back it up with a talent you have sharpened and heightened.

Believe in yourself, and also believe in your audience. They'll let you know how far your talent can take you.

Don't be discouraged if a positive reaction isn't immediate. Most comedians spend many years practicing and polishing their acts before they actually make a living in this business. Be prepared for the disappointments, but be aware of any gradual improvement you make, too. If you can honestly say you're getting better, then continue to work hard. If not, then don't be afraid to reevaluate your career choice.

Know your options. Remember, good comedy writers and people who are knowledgeable about the business angle are also in demand within the entertainment industry.

Never fall into the trap of being content to remain at one level. Always strive to push your talent as far as it will take you. For example, some comedians who are successful at the open-mike level feel comfortable and stay there for years doing the same act. I don't recommend such a career. Have a goal within your reach that will further your career, and do your best to achieve it.

Good luck, have fun, do your homework, and, most importantly, keep laughing.

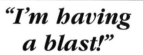

"I'm having a blast!"

DREW CAREY

TALKING
AND
JOKING
WITH
WORKING
COMICS

11 Nice People to Deal with or The Drew Carey Technique

"The last time I went back to Cleveland, people were always stopping me and getting my autograph. It was like being famous."

DREW CAREY

Being loyal to your hometown is not a new concept. For some it's a way of life. For others, a new residence in a different location can be looked at as a fresh start or an escape from the past.

Drew Carey has the best of both worlds. He's moved into the upper echelon of Hollywood's comedy industry without ever taking his heart far from his hometown. In fact, he visits his old stomping grounds practically every day on the set of his sitcom. The star of ABC's *The Drew Carey Show* has turned the tables on those who once used Cleveland, Ohio, as the punchline for too many feeble jokes and has invited viewers to laugh with him about life in his city.

"I don't know of any sitcom that was ever set in Cleveland," he told me. "Especially one that makes it a point to let everybody know it's from Cleveland. That's the thing about Clevelanders. They always have this chip on their shoulders. I do—I won't let anybody get away with it. I always correct people when they say something bad about Cleveland or make some kind of snide remark, which you hardly ever hear anymore. Once in a while you meet some idiot, and I always correct him."

Thanks to strong ratings and a solid production team, viewers across the country are tuning in to Carey's hometown every week. On his show, the comedian/writer/producer/co-creator works in the personnel department of a downtown Cleveland department store. A regular guy who enjoys a beer after work, Carey hangs around a local polka bar, belongs to a miserable car pool, and enjoys being with his neighborhood pals. Outside the store, his wardrobe is based on anything emblazoned with a Cleveland sports logo.

He started his stand-up career in Cleveland and probably would have never left except for his desire to achieve one goal:

"I wanted to do *The Tonight Show*," he said. "That was the only reason I moved out to Los Angeles in the first place."

"Since you're so loyal to Cleveland," I pointed out, "it must have been very hard for you to pack up and move."

"It was really tough," he answered. "I was crying the whole night before. I cleaned the whole house out. I never saw the house with all the kitchen cabinets and closets empty. No furniture! It was really depressing."

Carey has a reputation for working hard as a comedian and taking his career seriously. Years of dedication brought him a steady climb up through the comedy ranks and resulted in his success on television and in clubs. Since the groundwork of any established stand-up performer is a solid act with funny comedy material, I asked what writing tips he might have for new comedians.

Without taking a moment to think it over, he replied: "Write every day. I was doing this thing that really, really helped me, and I turned a couple of other people onto this, and it really helps them out too. We would e-mail each other ten jokes a day—one-liner jokes. The idea was to get one joke a day for an average of five good ones a week. Ten a day is not that hard to do. Then, after you get going, it only takes you about twenty minutes to do. You just start ripping them out because you're so used to doing it. Ten jokes a day, even if you don't get any that day out of the ten that are any good.

Drew Carey and the author backstage at the Improv.

"Say they're obviously ten bad jokes," he continued. "Don't sweat it. You might get two good jokes the next day. Or three the day after that. You just want five a week, and if you time it out with a setup, punchline, and laugh, it comes to almost an hour a year of new material! It's so easy to do.

"To make it tougher, they have to be clean and nontopical. You have to write ten clean, nontopical jokes a day. When I say nontopical, I mean you can't do: 'Gee, did you hear what happened in Bosnia today?' They have to be jokes that can last a couple of years.

"Talk about supercharging your act and your brain! For one thing, you let yourself know you can. So you feel like, 'Boy, I am talented and I am funny' because you think of these jokes. And ignore the jokes that don't work. You write ten just to get that one.

"You also set your subconscious to think funny," he observed. "You'll think of extra jokes all during the day, once you get going. After a few weeks, you'll be walking down the street and 'oh!'—another joke will come to you. Something will just come to you out of the blue. I'm telling you, it really works, and everybody I recommend it to raves about it. Blake Clark, a frequent co-star on the show, hasn't missed a day since I told him the 'Drew Carey technique.' As long as you give me credit for it, spread the gospel: It's a great way to keep yourself fresh.

"Sometimes I write jokes and don't even use them," he continued. "But I used a couple on *The Tonight Show* during my last spot, because I hadn't been on the road as much since I started my show."

Ah, the veteran comedian's dream come true, a sitcom and a home life, rather than the hardships of the road. But since performing can be addictive to those who do it well, I asked Carey if he still had any opportunities to do live shows.

"Hardly at all anymore, because I haven't got the time," he answered.

"Does that bother you?"

"Yeah," he admitted. "I work twelve to fifteen hours a day on the show, so I don't really have time to do anything else."

My inquiring mind started racing. It sounded a lot like show-*business* to me. I asked if he was becoming more of a businessman instead of a comedian. "No," he replied. "I just added that part. It's certainly on my mind all the time. I never thought I'd be talking about demographics and stuff like that!

"You have to be really professional and businesslike. Some comics forget when they show up late, or treat the waitresses bad, trash a condo, run up a big bar bill—that kind of stuff. That's not the way to go. Even talk that's rude, getting on the phone and bad-mouthing other club owners. You don't know if that guy knows the other guy, or that woman knows the other woman, or one comic likes another comic as a person. You know," he advised, "I know so many guys who aren't that funny, but they always 'middle' or MC all the time because they're just nice people to deal with."

"It must be mind-boggling to remain a nice person with the sudden fame from a television show," I commented.

He responded quickly: "I think being famous and getting all this money frees you to be whatever you've been holding back, to be what you naturally are. So, if you're naturally a jerk, you can stop being nice to people you don't want to be nice to anymore. You can start speaking your mind like you always wished you could have. If you feel like being a total bitch, a whiner and complainer, unappreciative of everything that God's given you, then you can! You can start demanding stuff, like, 'Where's my limo?' because you're naturally a jerk.

"If you're naturally a nice person, it still frees your ego to do whatever it wants. Well, I'm always nice to everybody, I think. It's more important to me to be decent to people, because I've got to sleep at night. I don't want people writing articles about me saying, 'That Drew was a real jerk today.' I don't want to name any names, but I've heard horrible stories about people who get famous. One was on a sitcom, and all people could talk about was how awful this guy was. He was mean to everybody, nasty and demanding. Then you read the same thing about people who are brand-new, getting their first taste of fame.

"You had some sitcom experience earlier, on a show called *The Good Life*," I noted. "How did the TV roles compare with your stand-up act?"

"Actually, TV's always going to be watered-down," Carey admitted. "Everybody's watered-down from the stage, even Jerry Seinfeld and Tim Allen, the biggest former stand-ups on television today! There's no way their television shows will ever be as funny as they themselves are doing stand-up.

"First of all, stand-up comedy has no story to it," he explained. "When you have to put a story in it and other characters that you have to serve, right then you're dead—if you only want to do your stand-up act. Because it doesn't translate, you know?"

"Is it fun having your own sitcom?" I asked for those of us who can only tune in and imagine.

"Oh, yeah, I'm having a blast!" he laughed.

"You own a house in Cleveland. Any plans to retire in your hometown?"

"Yes. I plan to go there as much as I can," he answered. "Which is hardly ever because I'm always in Los Angeles working. I'm going to have the house fixed up so I can fly back on the weekends, spend the weekend there, and get refreshed. Tim Allen gave me that advice. We went to Las Vegas together, and I said, 'Any advice?' He said, 'Yeah, get a house in Cleveland.' I said, 'Really? I already did that!' He said it really saved him the first few seasons of *Home Improvement,* going back to Detroit. He would go to his home and connect.

"I'm taking lessons from people like Tim Allen and Jay Leno," he added. "They're *good* people to take advice from. You read stories about other people on shows and how horrible they are to work with. Then you talk to people who work on those shows and you realize those stories are true. You think, 'Boy, I don't want to act like that.'"

12 Packing for Success or Making an Extreme Understatement by Calling Him Loud

"If you took NyQuil and No-Doz at the same time, would you dream you couldn't sleep?"

CARROT TOP

One Saturday night, I received a call from two comedian friends who live and work out of New York City. It was a conference call so I could get the full effect of how well they work together. Between laughs and attempts at new material, they talked about how great the comedy scene is on the East Coast and about how funny they are. But one thing kept crossing my mind. If they're so funny, what were they doing sitting home on a Saturday night, the busiest night of the week for a comedy club?

They went on about who's funny, who's not, old acts, new acts, and the politics that go into finding performing time in the Big

118

Apple. Finally, I had to interrupt them with some cold, hard facts that came out sounding not too subtle.

"Guys," I told them in my best Professor Irwin Corey voice, "not too long ago, I saw one of the most popular acts in comedy. He's breaking down old barriers, setting different standards, and attracting new audiences to live comedy shows. So far, nothing you're telling me comes even remotely close to doing that."

Two quick gasps registered through the long-distance line that told me I had struck a nerve. It was followed by a unison challenge for me to explain my daring statement. "Carrot Top," I answered, knowing that if we lived in a cartoon world, my answer would be written in bold orange letters in a big bubble over my smiling face.

My two friends made some minor protests concerning the cerebral, observational comedy they so cleverly weave into monologues to make an audience think. Before they were done, I had to interrupt again.

"That's fine, for *you*," I said, "but don't limit yourselves or expect the expected. The last thing you want to be is inventory in a factory outlet for cloned comedians. Carrot Top's show is the result of the comedy boom of the mid-'80s catching up with today's MTV generation, then kicking it up another notch. You may have different opinions from the many comics who already talk about airline food and convenience stores, but you'd better have a style of delivery that will make me want to listen. Otherwise, I might be more interested in the club's menu or why my tablemates have broken down into small discussion groups."

Silence from the New York end of the conversation—so I proceeded to tell them that Carrot Top, the master of prop comedy, is *big,* in performance, style, originality, and popularity. Every few years the entertainment business is shaken up by something new and different that grabs an audience and changes ideas that have been carved in stone since—well, the last big turnaround. Think back to some of the performers with the biggest impact on their generation, look at what was going on before them, and you'll have no problem realizing this. In the comedy world, many acts were known for being risqué on certain stages, but toned down their material to reach larger audiences in upper-class clubs, concerts, films, television, and recordings. Then Lenny Bruce, and later, George Carlin and Richard Pryor came on the scene and paved the way for comics to use totally uninhibited language and in whatever medium they were performing. Some trends come and go, but those who remain in the spotlight seem to be the ones that continue to grow and create while remaining true to their original vision. Whether they're saying something serious or just for good fun, they won't be satisfied until they reach the next plateau.

One of the true players in the comedy world who defied the prevailing standards of his time and reinvented the idea of a live comedy show is Carrot Top. The wildly colorful jokester has done away with the traditional lone

Carrot Top gets an idea for another funny prop. (Photo by Deborah Triplett)

microphone, barren stage, and single spotlight to give the word "show" new meaning in stand-up. His vision was closer to rock 'n' roll with solid laughs than to anything done before, and proof of his success came in 1994 when he was named Comedian of the Year by the American Comedy Awards.

The large theater where I witnessed his latest comedic explosion had been transformed into a loony bin, and I didn't see an empty seat. When entering a venue for a performance by Carrot Top, you're normally greeted by pounding rock music and a stage filled with backdrops, side-drops, lasers, fog machines, brightly painted travel trunks, and lots of color. A member of Carrot Top's management team assured me that a psychedelic road show from 1970 was not in town, and that I had the right ticket. Today's pop entertainment, paralleling society, has developed a loud, in-your-face immediacy. My own term for what we experienced that night would be "Heavy Metal Rock 'n' Roll Comedy."

"Yeah!" exclaimed Carrot Top when I threw that description at him. "That's what I'm trying to do. Something a little different. My hero is George Carlin, but people like him do just the opposite of what I do, and I would never be as good as George Carlin or some of my other idols. (At least I don't *think* I'd be as good as them.) So I wanted to do something a little different."

Carrot Top's performance was a two-hour extravaganza. Everything onstage seemed to smoke, flash, and almost come alive the moment he walked out to the audience's cheers. It was as if Keith Richards had hit the first chords of "Brown Sugar," and that's not where the similarities end. The audience, like the ones for the Rolling Stones, has grown up. Sure, there were kids in tie-dye, but I also saw many gray heads and suits prepared for a night of laughter.

"From day one, I said I was going to have a big show and play theaters. All the comics would say, 'Whadya mean play *theaters?* First you gotta have

fans, you gotta have an act!'" he laughed. "I said that one day that's what I'd
do. They would all make fun of me. So I had a strobe light, and I'd do silly
things with that. I'd have music, and these things that people would laugh at.
All the comics would make fun of me and say, 'What are you doing?' And I
said, 'I'm just doing something different. Why does everyone do the same
thing? I mean, I'm gonna take jokes, add lights, put music to it, and make it,
like . . . bizarre.'

"I couldn't even describe it. It was just gonna be rock 'n' roll kinda fun
comedy, as opposed to just standing there with a microphone."

"Sounds like you had the basic idea from the start," I commented. "Then
you just had to find your style."

"Exactly!" he agreed. "Defining myself and making myself stand out. But
also it would be something I would enjoy doing every night. To this day, I
really, thoroughly, can't wait to get onstage. The whole show energizes me.
When I hit the stage, I'm as completely ready as the crowd. I'm ready to go.

"When I first started doing comedy, I was always kind of silly in my own
little way, but the props just happened. It wasn't even something I'd thought
about. A lot of comics started with props and stuff like that. Probably the
second time I went onstage I had props. The first time, I just went on being
stupid."

"Where did you find the nerve to do that?" I asked.

"It was in Florida, when I was going to college at Florida Atlantic
University. You know, the Yale of the South!" he laughed. "I went onstage
and did George Carlin's and Steven Wright's jokes, and material of that
nature—just because I didn't know what I was doing. I went up there and
everybody said, 'Man, that was really funny, but those weren't your jokes,
were they?' And I said, 'No.' They said, 'You can't do that!'

"I didn't know why, and they told me I had to write my own jokes. But I
said that people do that with music—you know, 'Here's one from Jimmy
Buffett.' Why can't I do that? They said it doesn't work that way. So it was
back to the drawing board.

"The next time I went up with a few props. I remember one of them was a
Crime Watch sign, and I'd say, 'Check it out. I took a Crime Watch sign. I guess
they're not watching too good, 'cause I took their sign!' And I got this amazing
response; it got the energy of the room up. The next time I went up, I brought
about three or four more props. And I never looked back from there.

"I felt really comfortable," he continued. "It felt just like show and tell,
really. And I learned, even back then, to make this a big show. 'Cause I really
wanted to be a rock star. I'd think, 'God, I can't be a rock star. I don't know
how to play an instrument, I don't know how to sing. I'm screwed!'"

A rock 'n' roll comedy performance by Carrot Top is anything but subtle.
At first glimpse, you know he's an original and that his name fits perfectly.
His hair curls and waves in every direction and its color, if it were included
in your crayon box, would be described as "brightest orange." His wardrobe

does nothing to offset the color shock, and if I only said it was loud, I'd be committing an extreme understatement. He may wear a floral patterned vest, suspenders, tie-dye—as long as it's bursting with colors.

"I was always kinda weird, anyhow," he explained. "I never really thought about my attire, I was just being me. But people made a big deal about it, saying I dress kinda clown-like, and nothing matches.' And I thought, 'Well, this is how I dress!' For comedy purposes it worked out great."

I pointed out that in New York we used to joke that no one wanted to follow an act with an accordion, a monkey, whatever! I asked: "Didn't some of the more traditional stand-ups give you grief about the props?"

"Oh, tons of it!" he laughed. "But when I was playing the clubs I liked it that people didn't want to follow me. I always went last. It didn't bother me because I had a lot of energy and was different. But I also had a lot of comics that would love to open for me, because we would have big crowds. They would say, 'Hey, as long as I don't have to follow all that crap, I'll go before you!'

"What I do is different from the true stand-up comic's art form, which is why I don't even consider myself a stand-up comic. I say I'm a jokester, I'm a physical comic, and I make people laugh. I don't analyze every word I say. I don't look at myself as a true monologuist. I look at myself as an entertainer. I can go up there and just have fun, you know?

"So when comics say, 'Carrot Top, he's not a stand-up comic.' I say, 'You're right! I'm not!' What they do is a whole different art form. It's standing there, you and your microphone and your soul. What I do is go out of control. It's me being silly, being wacky. A kind of physical funny, as opposed to the type where every word, every little phrase is structured. I just go up there and talk from my heart."

Carrot Top's comedy material needs little explanation. You get the joke, or you don't. Either way, it doesn't matter, because he wastes little time moving on to the next one. He'll drag a trunk to the center of the stage, open it up, and begin pulling out inventions made from household items that are truly absurd. It was obvious each item had been given a lot of thought. Each is explained and demonstrated to the howling crowd.

Two quick examples: a Frisbee with a dog already attached, and a coat covered with smoke alarms for someone trying to quit smoking. Each one seemed funnier than the one before. And there was not a dull moment in the show; the best description for his delivery, style, and stage antics would be *rapid-fire*.

"Which is what I still try to do," he stated. "I try to keep it clever and fun, but you know, as comedy goes, you throw in some stuff that's real stupid and not very clever, and I tell the crowd that also. I say, 'Wow, that was really stupid!' And they like that. They like when I'm honest with them.

"It's like Carlin," he pointed out. "He's one of the only guys left, I think, who's absolutely brilliant. And he'll talk about abortion or the death penalty for, like, twenty minutes and you're on the edge of your seat just thinking, 'My God, I can't believe what he's saying!' And then he'll say, 'Now, let's talk about farts!' What?! And it's funny, because he pulls you right into it."

"It's obvious a lot of thought goes into your material," I remarked. "Isn't it true that you refer to your props as inventions?"

"You know why I do?" he asked. "Because a prop to me is just a prop without any kind of joke attached to it—just a basketball, a flower, a vase, or a coffeepot. Whereas the invention I do would be a coffeepot with something attached to it, or something made out of it, so there's been an invention to it. For instance, paper cups would be just props. But when you put them together with string, then it becomes an invention. It's not just cups anymore."

"Was it like that from the beginning with you?" I wondered. "Inventions rather than just props?"

"Yes, exactly. I had my own style of prop comedy. In fact, a lot of comics such as Jerry Seinfeld, Gary Shandling, Bill Maher, a lot of guys I respect and love, have come up to me and said, 'You know why I like you? Because your stuff is creative. It's not just a newspaper you're holding up, it's a newspaper with a clear window in it so you can watch your kids and still read the paper.' Or something. That's not a prop of mine, but I'm just thinking!"

"I have a guy who helps me build the stuff, and he comes to the show every night. After the show we go through what we're gonna make, or what did good and what didn't, and what to improve on. That's the key to it, seriously, just to work. It's like anything else: You've got to be working on it constantly or it goes away. And I think people can tell. They'll say, 'He hasn't been working on new stuff.'"

Carrot Top also played by different rules when it came to finding his style and working out his act on various stages. Instead of becoming a fixture on the comedy-club circuit, he made his reputation in the college market.

"I never really did the club scene that long," he said. "Instead of doing the clubs and my five minutes a night, I went to colleges and did thirty-five to forty minutes a night and built my act that way. It polished my act doing the real thing on the road.

"That's when it all started, because I was doing a lot of colleges, 250 or 300 different colleges in one year. I worked my butt off! I don't think I stopped touring for two years. I played every college I know and built my little following. Then there was word of mouth. People would say, 'This Carrot Top guy, you gotta see him.' Then I started doing television and I'd get the college kids and their parents. The parents would say, 'I saw this Carrot Top guy.' And the kids would say, 'We saw him at college.' Then they'd hear I was coming to town, and I'd get both the college people and the older people. It was really neat."

"In 1994 you won Comedian of the Year at the American Comedy Awards," I reminded him. "Did that change things for you?"

"It was definitely a legitimizing feeling," he answered. "It really made me feel like I've really done something of stature. I remember that when they first started doing those awards I was just getting into comedy, and I'd watch that show. And to win that thing—wow!—it was amazing, because they did the voting on Comedy Central. It was very gratifying because it wasn't the industry or the comics who were voting, it was just the people, the fans. And I was up against *amazing* talent! I mean, so much that I demanded a recount. There's no way I'd won that damn thing!

"It was interesting that I did win," he continued, "and for what my act was about. Basically, it meant people wanted to see what I was doing or liked what I was doing. There's a lot of people who look at the dark humor out there and think, 'I just don't get it.' I just try to make it where it's fun for everybody, as opposed to political or heavy or deep. It's just fun."

A Carrot Top performance ends with a wild montage of musical impressions ranging from Willie Nelson to Madonna and just about everyone in between. Backed by a medley of songs blasted from the sound system, the performer uses wigs and more props to become every school kid's version of those artists, with his own observations thrown in: U-2's "Still Haven't Found What I'm Looking For" was defined by a flashlight searching through the darkened stage; Michael Jackson's "Beat It"—well, read the tabloids about that one; and his manic Mick Jagger left the stage as the crowd roared.

"I love adding music to it because everyone relates to music. I've had a lot of people say to me after the show, 'I loved all the music!' You know, most comics don't put any music in their show, and I *love* music."

How did he get the name Carrot Top?

"Well, the good ones were taken," he laughed. "It was one of those things where I had been called so many nicknames, and, believe it or not, I was a marketing major. The name Scott Thompson was taken by a comic actor, so I decided to go with something that's marketable to a certain degree, and kinda fun. As far as marketing is concerned, it goes along with my show.

"The first time someone across campus yelled, 'Hey, Carrot Top!' I thought, 'Oh Lord, do I really wanna do this to myself?!' But now it's second nature," he laughed.

As for my buddies in New York, the ones I lectured that Saturday night on the phone, I don't assume they're going to go raid their local toy store, but they can consider themselves warned. In the world of comedy, we don't know where, when, or how, but there will be a future. It belongs to whoever has the nerve, like Carrot Top, to open the next door.

Put Yourself in the Stand-Up Spotlight
or
That's What We Call Dues

"I'm in the grocery store with my four-year-old daughter. There's a big lady in the aisle in front of us. My daughter says, 'Daddy, pass her.' I said, 'We can't pass this lady. She's a big lady. She's got little skinny ladies orbiting around her.' My daughter says, 'Pass her!' The lady had a beeper. The beeper goes off and my four-year-old says, 'Careful, Daddy, she's backing up!'

BOBBY COLLINS

Funny material, hard work, stage experience, acting skills, and a healthy dose of personality have never hurt anyone's comedy career. Take a look at Bobby Collins, one of today's most consistently employed comedians. His stand-up work has never been limited to a nightclub's stage; his résumé boasts appearances in films and sitcoms, host of *VH-1's Stand-Up Spotlight,* and national recognition through numerous television commercials.

He earns his "Mr. Personality" label the minute he walks into a comedy club. He can talk about almost anything and make it funny. It's not uncommon to see everyone around him laughed-out before he even begins a show.

Collins's audiences often request their favorite comedy bits. At a recent show, I listened as he delivered the goods, but at his own pace. The first mention of his loyal dog brought applause of anticipation from certain audience members and a scolding from him that they watch way too much TV. What made the act particularly interesting was the comic's ability to switch gears and take the expected story in a new, unfamiliar direction. He would then wrap up the bit with what they wanted to hear. That shows why having plenty of experience is so important to any comedy career.

It's difficult to get that experience if you don't get jobs, and one of the ways to get that job is through good promotional material. The more professionally you're presented to bookers, the more professionally you'll be treated. I spoke with Collins about two of the most important promotional tools for comedians.

"I use your headshot as an example in my workshop," I began. "It gives us an idea of who you are, what you are. Tell us about pictures."

"As a matter of fact, I just had new pictures made. Now the price goes up. The more popular you are, the higher the price. Same pictures! You know what I mean?" he laughed.

"Pictures used to be, *used to* be, your calling card," he said, "Anywhere you went, you had to give them your picture. And, usually, on the back of your picture was your experience: Where you've played, who you are. That's changed! Now it's become the picture *and* the video. You don't know how many pictures and videos I've gotten because of *VH-1's Stand-Up Spotlight!*

"Most people don't understand that when you hand people your video, they don't want a twenty-minute act. They want not more than eight minutes, and they would prefer five. To give somebody an idea, a taste. Because we all know comedy! I can look at a tape for a minute-and-a-half and say: 'Put him under physical comedy. I like his movements.' Or 'He's cerebral. He stands still, he doesn't move, and he just runs jokes.' Or, 'He's a juggler' . . . or this or that. It's all in the presentation.

"So a video and picture now is your calling card," he said, "now that video has become more important with the advent of VH-1, MTV and all these rock videos."

When someone sends him a tape from a television show, instead of one taped in a club, it carries more weight, he thinks; it's higher up on the professional scale.

"That's why a lot of acts that have been on *The Tonight Show* like to use that tape. It's a lot more impressive than putting out a tape of "Comedy on the Road" or one that a friend shot at the local club. If I need one comic real quick, I'm gonna go with the guy who sent me the TV spot, even though the other guy might be a little funnier. Because I gotta go with what's proven."

I tested this premise a bit more: "If someone sends you a videotape that was shot from the back of a comedy club, and it's shaky, with not great audio, do you immediately fast-forward it, turn it off, or give it a shot?"

"You give it a quick shot," he answered, "but nine out of ten times those tapes are very foggy. You can hardly hear the guy and can't see what kind of club it's at. You also get a lot of haze in it. Usually it gets turned off and thrown right in the garbage."

"When you were hosting *VH-1's Stand-Up Spotlight,* did you still work with videotapes, or did your name carry you through the door?"

"Rosie O'Donnell is my friend, so when I got that show I didn't have to audition or anything. I had done five appearances before, and one of them had gotten me a cable award, because the show was selected as a really good show. When they were deciding who to pick, Rosie said, 'Why don't we go with Bobby?' They had picked someone else, but Rosie threatened to leave. She said, 'Whatayacrazy? Go with Bobby Collins! This show's all about personality!'"

The lesson there was that it pays to know the right people. Still wondering where videos had come in for his career personally, I ventured: "After you'd started in New York, did video help you get into the Los Angeles market and Budd Friedman's Improv there?"

"No. I didn't need a video because he could see me right there at the club," he replied, and he related how he'd gotten his audition with Friedman: "He had heard of me. He knows who's out there. He said, 'So, you're the guy from New York that a lot of comics are talking about!' It came pretty easy for me, because he said, 'Let's see what you've got. You want to do a set?' I said, 'Sure.' And he said, 'Okay, just sign up and call your avails to *you!* Call Dave and you're on!'

"The best way to encourage new comics," he said, "is to tell them: Work at your craft. It's stage time, stage time, that makes you good! And writing. You've got to do as much stage time and writing as possible. You will be found out, whether you're in Los Angeles or in Gaboo. It might take them a little longer to find you in Gaboo, but they'll find you. Why? Because the cream does rise to the top."

"How do you spell Gaboo?" I said, transcribing his words painstakingly.

"I don't know . . . G - A - boo!"

Somehow that triggered another nugget he passed along: "I get videotapes now, like the one a girl offered me the other night in a comedy club. She was opening for me, and she says, 'Hey, Bobby, can I getcha a tape?' And I said, 'Well, I'll be honest with you: Is it professionally made?' She says, 'Well, my friend taped it.' I said, 'Don't send it!'

"Don't send a tape until you've worked at a club, and I only know two, like Caroline's and Rascals, that have a television show. If you do those clubs, they'll tape it for you professionally, whether or not it's on their television shows, which have been cancelled now. They'll tape it there, and it looks good because they're using two cameras. But otherwise, *don't!* Why risk putting yourself out there saying, 'I got a tape. Naw, it's not so good'?

"It's like the comic who's not ready," he continued, "but he thinks he's really funnier and further along than he really is. And he gets up and he does his ten minutes and you think, 'The guy's not funny.' But he could have been nervous, or it could have been a bad audience! Yet you know as well as I do that someone like Budd is not going to see him for another year, or until he's got it. This guy's just wasted a whole year!

"And that's what we call dues," he added.

"It has changed now, with the videotape," he stated. "But most people still don't understand. Five minutes tops! For instance, there's a sitcom going up about a guy and his dog. The people who are casting it are telling me that they're saying, 'There's only one guy you should use. Bobby Collins! He talks about his dog! That's who he is!' The guy casting goes, 'I don't know . . . I don't know him. Get him in here!' Next thing you know, they ask for my tape, and I send that five-minute piece I did on VH-1. The five-minute piece on my dog and *bingo,* I'm there!"

"What else do you see happening in the business?" I asked, thinking that his dog could have a role after all.

"People are going for the whole sentiment thing," he observed. "It's going back to the family now. If it's nice, go with it. It's better than all that screaming. People are getting back to roots. Why? Because they're seeing in this country everything that's going on, and they're sick of it. So what makes people feel safe? We're going right back to the house, the home, relationships. You know what I mean? The car, walking, friends. . . . It makes people feel secure."

14

Hey, Hey, We're . . . a Hit! or Life in a Barrel of Monkees

"You know why cannibals don't eat clowns? Because they taste funny."

MICKY DOLENZ

Landing a regular part in a sitcom can be like a dream come true for many comedians. Fame, fortune, and a regular paycheck would be three popular wishes if you ever found the right magic lamp to rub.

But many former stars of the small screen have found themselves locked into their scripted personas and have a difficult time trying to break their public image from the mold. Some do it, while others don't. Once upon a time in the land of show-business, it was discovered that the union of comedy and music provided great entertainment. Comics sang and singers joked on stages and in films. Two well-known teams to prove this point: It's hard to find a Marx Brothers film that doesn't break into a musical interlude, and the Beatles' movies *A Hard Day's Night* and *Help!* showcased their comic abilities as well as their songs.

In 1966, almost a quarter-century before MTV, Hollywood decided to bring that sort of musical fun to television viewers on a weekly basis. A casting call went out for four young actors to fit the program's needs, and also for songwriters to supply the music for the grueling prime-time schedule. The results exceeded almost everyone's expectations. *The Monkees* scored as both a sitcom and record-selling phenomenon.

Micky Dolenz, Davy Jones, Peter Tork, and Mike Nesmith joked and sang their way through two seasons on the small screen and on numerous tours that attracted mobs of screaming fans. Songs such as "Last Train to Clarksville" and "I'm a Believer" were instant hits that still bring back fun memories and earn new fans, thanks to reruns and classic-rock radio.

In talking with Micky Dolenz about *The Monkees,* I learned that he has not spent his post-Monkee days waiting for the dream-come-true to return. He's gone on to successful careers as a painter and as a director while continuing to act and make music during occasional Monkee reunions.

"I'm either a renaissance man or a dilettante," he joked. "It depends on your perception. I suppose my biggest break in terms of career moves was after *The Monkees* was originally on the air. Around 1975, I went to England and started directing. I did that solid for about fifteen years. When anybody asks me on the street, or if I'm filling out a visa and it says 'Occupation,' I'll put *director*. That's what I consider my day job. I've done directing for many, many years, longer than I've done anything else.

"But I've done an awful lot of things and will continue to do so," he said. "Also, living in England for so long—over there, the lines of demarcation are not so heavily drawn. You can drift back and forth across different fields more easily than you can here in the States. We tend to lock people into one role.

"But, obviously, I'm a singer and an actor," he continued. "I also paint. I call my work Still Life of Things You Can't See. I'm a science groupie, and in England I was trying to get a degree in physics. I paint stuff that's seen through microscopes or through deep space telemetry; my art is based on those kind of images. I use some source material and my knowledge of science, but then I kind of make it up, impressions of what it would look like if you could see cell structure with your naked eye."

It sounded to me as if both careers would be enough to keep anyone busy. Since he continues to join forces with Davy and Peter as the Monkees for reunion tours, I asked:

"How does it feel to be a Monkee again after all these years?"

"In some ways it doesn't feel any different than it ever did," he said. "Getting back together periodically has become very timeless. You see, the Monkees are a lot more like the Marx Brothers than, say, the Beatles. The Marx Brothers didn't really hit their stride until they were in their fifties. A lot of great artists haven't."

"Come to think of it," I said, using my knowledge of American trivia, "I don't think Groucho Marx even made a movie until he was in his forties."

"You're absolutely right!" he agreed.

"Are you having fun?" I asked.

"Absolutely," he answered without any hesitation. "Probably more than ever before."

"Let me try to dispel some rumors," I said, working up a little nerve. "I've always heard that everything stopped because you guys didn't get along."

*Comedian
Micky Dolenz.*

"The relationship has always been like a sibling rivalry," he admitted. "So when you say 'not get along,' it's in that context—the way brothers will fight and compete. But there's an underlying love and affection that has always gone through it. We've all mellowed, we've aged, we've dealt with our demons. We've all gone through our various variations of the Dark Night of the Soul and come out on the other side still alive and grateful for it.

"And it isn't like we're desperate to do this," he added. "None of us is, which also helps. We can go out and sing the songs and have a good time. I think the audience picks up on that. When you look at the audience reaction, it's hard not to get pretty excited about it. It's not like we're having to sell this thing or shove it down people's throats or fire the audience up. We walk in, and they're screaming!"

After a good laugh he said, "For starters we of course do all the hits. That's most of the show right there. We don't do medleys. I think that reeks of Vegas lounge acts. We do a rock 'n' roll concert. I mean, I do," he laughed. "The others might do something else. We goof around a bit like the Monkees are wont to do. That's just the nature of the beast."

Paul McCartney has said that there are lines in certain songs that make him think of John Lennon, so I asked Dolenz if there were any memories from all those years ago that might come to his mind when the Monkees are performing now.

"No, it's not like that for me," he said. "We had to work so fast and were recording so much that I would, at times, do three lead vocals in a night. Which now is unheard of! They needed so much material for the show that we were really under the gun to go in and record."

We discussed the issues surrounding his moving beyond the Monkees.

"You have to understand that the Monkees were originally—from my perception—a television show about a rock 'n' roll group. I was an actor playing a part of a drummer named Micky. That character is not me any more than Leonard Nimoy is Mr. Spock. Over the years the association has gotten to the point where there's very little distinction made between the two. It bothers you when you can't move on in your life or your career. I've been fortunate, so it hasn't bothered me as much as if I had been stuck in Los Angeles trying to get work as an ex-Monkee and not being able to.

"Just after *The Monkees*"—here Dolenz sounded as if he didn't enjoy the memory much—"I remember going to acting interviews, and they would say, 'What are you doing here? We don't need any drummers.' That's while going for an acting interview!

"A lot of the problem lies in the fact that people want you in a certain pigeonhole. They aren't prepared to accept you in any other capacity. They don't want to. Not only the public, but the media. It's comfortable for them. *This* person does *this,* and that's all they want to talk about. . . . It's not something you can get bitter or angry about, because you've got to be grateful for your success in the first place. Then, if you can, you try to change.

"I always imagine it like this big train that you started rolling," he said. "You know, by virtue of your own hard work, you get this train rolling, and it's your career. It gets rolling but suddenly it leaves without you! You're running along behind it forever, shouting, 'Wait for me!'"

"That was an awfully big train you were on in the 1960s," I said.

"At times I've gotten very annoyed by it. I've tried to get people to accept me or, rather, even be interested in anything else about my life. If I was somebody who had absolutely nothing else going, it might be different. But over the years I've mellowed, and the fact that I do have another real life helps a lot."

15

A Million Things Going on at Once or All I Know Is, It Works

"You know why you don't have a girlfriend? Because you play with dolls."

PEANUT THE WOOZLE, TO JEFF DUNHAM

One of the most popular comedy shows traveling the country today involves a talking "Woozle," a jalapeño-on-a-stick, a grumpy old man ,and a worm in the bottom of a tequila bottle. Oh, and there's one other attraction that goes with those characters: Jeff Dunham, the man who brings them all alive as a comedian/ventriloquist extraordinaire.

Dunham is known as one of the hardest-working entertainers on the concert and television circuit. He's the only person ever to win the prestigious Ventriloquist of the Year Award twice, and he was voted Best Male Stand-Up Comedian of the Year by the American Comedy Awards. He has also appeared on *The Tonight Show* more than any other ventriloquist and earned major show-biz notoriety by being one of only four comedians ever invited during his very first appearance on the show to sit on the couch next to Johnny Carson.

Dunham began performing at the age of seven, and his career has continued to grow. He'd gained quite a bit of show-biz experience by the time he reached his thirties—that and legions of fans. While he was on a recent tour, I discussed with him his work on the road and his life as a ventriloquist. Since I can't resist an opening, my first question had to be, "Are your lips moving right now?"

*Comedian Jeff
Dunham and
friends.*

"Absolutely not!" he countered.

"That's amazing," I said.

"I'm brilliant!" he answered. "In fact, I'm not even here doing this. I'm across town!"

Okay, I may occasionally be able to see an opening, but a good comic can always take it a step further. But instead of trading more setups, I asked him how he had put his talent for voices and characters together into such a popular act.

"I'm not the usual comedian that comes from a twisted background where my parents beat me or anything like that," he admitted. "I'm not your typical 'show-biz' person."

"*Dysfunctional* doesn't fit in anywhere as a descriptive word?" I asked.

"It's like Robin Williams," he said. "He grew up in a nice, upper middle-class family where everything was fine. That's the way it was for me. The only thing that was halfway weird was that I didn't have any brothers or sisters. And I don't know whether this had much influence on it, but there was no one there to discourage me from taking up an odd hobby. I got my first dummy when I was in the third grade, got books and records from the library, and started teaching myself. It's been an interesting, slow and steady progression upward. I've gone all the way from doing book reports in elementary school, to Cub Scout banquets and church shows. Then in junior high school, I started doing some corporate functions. Then on into high school and college—it just kept going up and up. It's been a really fun and long take-off ride."

"What was it like going to school with you? Were you always the class entertainer?" I wondered.

"You know," he said, "you hear that about guys who do what I do, and they still take advantage of the ability to 'throw their voice.' And I've done a few things—never too much. But even now people ask my wife: Does he make things talk? Does the cereal say things in the morning?' No!"

I wanted to know if it was difficult to teach yourself to be a ventriloquist from only books and records.

"Naw, when you're a kid," he laughed, "you can do anything, you've got all the time in the world. It's exactly like playing a musical instrument or a sport: The earlier you started, the better you are. When I hear about kids getting interested in it, I think it's great. If a twenty-five-year-old comes up to me and says, 'Hey, I'm gonna take up ventriloquism,' my immediate thought is, 'Have you eliminated every other possibility for a hobby?' It's very strange for an older person to get into it. I mean, it's fine, but when you start as a little kid, there's just an innate natural talent there that is developed."

Who inspired him to do this?

"Edgar Bergen, when I was younger, just because he was the only person I could find anything written about or any audiocassettes on," he said. "He was the most famous ventriloquist in America, as well as the world. Also he's a big inspiration to me now, but not because he was a great ventriloquist—he was a horrible ventriloquist. Technically he was awful. What he was great at were the characterizations of Charley McCarthy and Mortimer Snerd and making them vivid. And the proof of that is, he was a ventriloquist on the radio! The fact is, the jokes were funny, the personalities were there, and for all the Americans sitting home on Sunday night listening to the radio, they truly believed Charley was a living and breathing person. Some of the historical writings are interesting, because people actually thought there was a little boy pretending to be a ventriloquist's dummy. Which is a huge compliment! Candice Bergen said Charley had a bigger room than she did while growing up, and nicer clothes."

"Do you consider yourself to be a comedian first, or a ventriloquist?" I asked, trying unsuccessfully not to move my lips.

"It used to be just a ventriloquist," he answered, "But very early on, after moving out to Los Angeles and getting into the big leagues, I realized that nobody really cares as much about the skill as they do about just sitting there and being entertained and laughing. To me, it's like juggling. You can watch a great juggler for about five minutes, and he can do x amount of things—'Gee, that's amazing!'—and it lasts for maybe three or four minutes. What, are you gonna throw five chainsaws in the air? The juggler who's entertaining to me is one who tells jokes, and even if he's a bad juggler, if he's funny I'll watch him five times as long as I will the good one who doesn't say anything.

"It's the same with ventriloquism. I pride myself in being technically good at what I do, but at the same time the most important thing is to make everybody laugh. The people who keep coming back to the show and bringing their friends are not there because I'm a good ventriloquist and don't move my lips, but because the characters are very vivid. The comedy is there. The so-called relationships between me and the puppets, and between the puppets themselves, are very real and believable. To me, my act has turned into a sitcom where the characters have their unique personalities."

I asked what advice he would have for young comedians or ventriloquists.

"For comedians," he answered, "it's such a long row to hoe, because comedy has taken such a nose-dive. For ventriloquists, there's so much work right now for people who have a different twist on stand-up. The jugglers, the magicians, and the ventriloquists, were looked down on and laughed at back in the early '90s. But you talk to club owners and that's the kind of stuff that sells now. There's a whole generation of people that have never seen 'variety.' They've never seen a good ventriloquist. They think it's something new and different, and they're coming to see it. Then, of course, the real money's in corporate work, and anybody who has a good, clean show will work their entire lives. I always try to keep my show rated PG or PG-13."

Dunham described the characters by way of explaining how a one-man comedy team like himself writes for his 'sitcom': "Walter, the old grumpy guy, certainly has his own spin on life; he's the dark side of comedy. Peanut is at the opposite end of the spectrum, the bright side of comedy. José, the jalapeño-on-a-stick, is just some weird icon that has some sort of cult following," he laughed. "A jalapeño-on-a-stick and people go bananas! I don't get that!"

"How did you think of these guys?" I asked. "What was the inspiration?"

"Growing up, I had your typical little wooden boy dummy that sits on your knee. Typical stuff," he explained. "And my whole life, I wanted to do something a bit different. I didn't want to be the typical ventriloquist that copies Edgar Bergen. One day, right about the time I graduated college, I just came up with Peanut—just a purple guy with green hair and brown fur and one shoe and, I don't know, his personality and his voice, it all just fit together.

"Walter was a complete accident. I saw a grumpy puppet somewhere and thought, 'That would be funny for two or three minutes in the act.' So I made a frowning doll, and he suddenly took off. Within the corporate world and the 'real' show-business world, he strikes a funnybone in a lot of people. I think it's because it's something completely different; nobody's had anything like this before."

"Is it true that Walter told Johnny Carson that it's gonna be a cold day in hell before he ever comes back to *The Tonight Show?*" I asked, before my lips could think about moving.

"Yeah!" he laughed, either at the memory or my mumbling. "It's a strange license, if you want to call it that, but you can say, or have the puppets say, the most outlandish things, and it makes people laugh. That wasn't the most outrageous thing he's ever said. It's not so much what he said, but to *whom*. If a real live person had said that to Johnny Carson, there would have been gasps or silence! The network would have gone to color bars, and the person would have been escorted from the stage. Whereas when it came out of Walter, it was very funny. I don't understand it, I don't get it. All I know is, it works, and it's real therapy for me."

As he continued to laugh, I agreed with his earlier notion of a sitcom surrounding him onstage. It must feel like he's wearing a lot of different hats to write for all these characters—among whom he sometimes has amazing six-way conversations that have become his trademark. "I try to write keeping that in mind," he answered. "That's what I really concentrate on.

"Some people don't realize that you're not only doing comedy, not only doing ventriloquism, but you're also acting as yourself, usually as the straight man. At the same time, you're having to act through the puppet, and they have to act themselves to be realistic. It's like playing golf. You're out there swinging a club and hoping you're holding it right, doing everything right— it's a million things going on at once."

"Every once in a while," he added, "I'll try to throw in a joke myself, and it goes nowhere!"

"But you open your shows alone, with just comedy," I protested.

"I do my own stand-up at first, to get to know the audience, and so they can figure out that I'm a person, too," he said. "I do that for about the first ten minutes. Yeah, I get decent laughs doing my own straight stuff. But when Walter or Peanut are out there, and I try to throw my own joke in, it's like the audience gives me that feeling of, 'Oh, come on, you're not funny!'"

"It's really interesting. You pull out an inanimate object, and it gets a bigger round of applause, which is strange. Another thing that gets me is when Walter says he's been married for forty-seven years and *that* gets a round of applause. How goofy is that?!"

Since we only had time for one more question, I laid aside my ventriloquist notions and fired away, now working my mind and lips together: "Since you travel so much," I said, "do you have any horror stories about working on the road?"

"There's one that always comes to mind," he said. "Every comedian has an arsenal of ad-libs, which is kind of a misnomer because an ad-lib is something that comes off the top of your head. But every comedian has them in his back pocket, ready to strategically place them anywhere in the show and make himself look like a genius. I've been doing this so long that I've seen and heard just about everything and I'm pretty much ready to handle anything that goes on with an audience.

"Well, I was in Dallas at the Improv, and there, in the second row, was a small person, a midget, who had come to see the show with his friend. And he had kept drinking a lot during the show, and a couple of times he popped off to Peanut. I had a couple of comeback lines, but really, what I am I gonna do, pick on the guy? So, finally, he got really obnoxious and Peanut slammed him with one good ad-lib, and it got a really big laugh. And this guy jumped up on top of his table and mooned us! No drunken, mooning midget ad-lib was in my arsenal. It was one of the few times both Peanut and I just stood there in silence. I really couldn't figure out what to say.

"Now," he laughed, "I have ad-lib lines ready. Not that I really bothered to write a drunken, mooning midget ad-lib line. I don't think in anyone's career that will happen twice!"

16 You Might Be a Comedian or Look out the Window!

"I'm wearing sting-ray boots. Blue sting-ray boots. And these boots make a statement: Never give a redneck money."

JEFF FOXWORTHY

In the entertainment industry, a crossover artist is someone who can appeal to separate audience groups. For instance, a singer specializing in gospel music might score a hit in the area of pop. When it comes to comedy crossover artists, there's Jeff Foxworthy. He's first and foremost a comedian, the top-selling comedy artist in recording history. His first CD, *You Might Be a Redneck If . . .*, sold more than 3 million copies—the only time a comedy album has ever reached that level of sales. He followed this with the release of a single and video for "Redneck Stomp," and another CD, *Games Rednecks Play,* which passed the 2-million mark in sales and earned him a Grammy nomination for Best Comedy Album.

Foxworthy has gone on to publish nine bestselling books. Some of their titles, such as *You Might Be a Redneck If . . .*, *Red Ain't Dead, Check Your Neck,* and *Redneck Classics,* might give you an idea that there's a theme to some of his projects. And of course, he has starred in sitcoms for both ABC and NBC, as well as in specials on HBO and Showtime. He's made regular appearances on *The Tonight Show with Jay Leno* and *The Late Show with David*

Letterman. He was also voted Comedian of the Year by the Nashville Network (TNN) for three years in a row.

Nashville, the home of country music, honoring comedians? That's what I mean about crossover artists. Foxworthy has found his niche not only in the world of comedy, but also as one of the favorites in the country-music industry. His third CD, *Crank It Up: The Music Album,* which also sold millions, featured a hit single with the band Little Texas called "Party All Night." The single "Games Rednecks Play," with country superstar Alan Jackson, earned them a Grammy nomination for Best Vocal Collaboration. Foxworthy has been a co-host for the televised Academy of Country Music Awards. And talk about crossovers: With Redneck Foods, he's opening a chain of Jeff Foxworthy barbecue restaurants and a line of barbecue sauces.

"It's kind of funny," he laughed, "because I didn't grow up listening to country. Well, a little bit, but mostly it was rock 'n' roll. Then when I first got into comedy, I had to do a few opening acts for rock 'n' roll shows. It was just horrible. I wouldn't even make it to the microphone without people throwing cups of beer at me. It was always: *'Hey, ya wanna raise hell?!'*

"'Yeahhh!'" he continued, doing a great impression of a rock-rowdy audience. *"'Ya wanna rock 'n' roll?!!' 'Yeahhh!' 'Okay,* but first . . . *a comedian!'*

"The day I decided I was never doing *that* again, I was working at Daytona Beach, after the band Poison and before the Hawaiian Tropic Bikini Contest," he said, laughing at the memory. "I was making big dough too, like sixty bucks, and we're just getting pelted with beers out on the beach. I thought, 'No, I don't need the money this bad.'

"Not long after that, I was playing in Savannah, Georgia, where Emmy Lou Harris was doing a show. Somebody who was opening for her got sick, so they called the club to see if anybody could come down, work clean, and do fifteen minutes before Emmy Lou. The club said, 'Foxworthy can do it.' I'd learned that comics require people to sit and listen, and they don't in rock 'n' roll, but this crowd did that. I walked away thinking, 'This is my audience.' From then on, I started working more and more country shows.

"To show you how little I knew," he recalled, "it was before the country boom and I didn't know the other two acts. I was the opening act and I went back and told my wife, 'These other two guys were pretty good.' The middle act was Vince Gill, and the headliner was Garth Brooks, and we were performing for a bunch of hairdressers! That'd be a pretty good show nowadays."

Foxworthy started his comedy career in Atlanta when he quit his $30,000-a-year job with IBM to hit the club circuit. His humor brought him a huge television-watching, record-buying, and ticket-purchasing audience, and the friendliness in his voice, flavored with an accent that more than reveals his Southern roots, makes listeners feel comfortable whether he's in a one-on-one conversation or standing in front of an arena full of fans.

Jeff Foxworthy and the author backstage at Cleveland's Palace Theatre.

"I was with IBM for five years," he said, "and have been doing comedy professionally for fourteen. But I was a road dog. I would go to L.A. and work a little bit, and I would go to New York and work a little bit. I used to have arguments in New York because people would say, 'If you were here every night, you could get discovered.' But I chose to be on the road and make a good living for a decade where nobody knew my name."

Eventually, everybody did know his name—and his redneck theme. "I do feel very fortunate that there was something people could hang their hat on and remember my name," he said. "There are hundreds of funny people in this country, and people in comedy clubs who can make you gut-laugh for an hour. But, for whatever reason, you leave and an hour later you're saying, 'What was that guy's name?' And I can go through airports and people will say, 'Oh, that's the redneck guy!'"

"How did you happen to fall into that?" I asked. "Comics are always looking for something to write about, and the redneck material turned out to be pretty original."

"When I first started to go into New York," he answered, "the only advice I ever got was that I needed to take voice lessons to get rid of my accent. It was like the old joke," he laughed, as he broke into a stereotypical Brooklynese: "'Hey, ya got a stoopid accent!' And I thought, 'Well, how come nobody up here is losing *their* accent? I mean it was good-natured, but they were always kidding me: 'You're nothing but an ol' redneck from Georgia,' and this and that. Then one week I was working in a Michigan club, and after the show we were around the bar, and it was, 'You're just an ol' Georgia redneck.' And that club was attached to a bowling alley that had valet parking. I'm watching people valet-park their pickup trucks at the bowling alley, and I said, 'You think you don't have rednecks? Look out the window!'

"I went back to the hotel room," he laughed, "and worked from the premise that there are rednecks all over this country, but a lot of people don't realize that's what they are. Back at the club the next night, I did this new set, and it worked from the first night I ever said it. I didn't think at the time that this was a hook. All I remember is that the jokes would work so well. I'd be in these 'comedy condos,' and I'd try to see how many of these I could come up with. I got up to about a hundred, and I'd have them all typed out, and I'd let the guys I was working with for the week read them. I kept thinking, 'You know, maybe I'll try to put this together as a book.'

"I enjoy your books," I said honestly.

"Well, most people keep them on the back of the toilet," he remarked with a laugh. "I can't tell you how many dozen comics told me, 'That's a really stupid idea.' Now I'll see them somewhere on the road, and they'll come up and say, 'Don't ever listen to my advice. What do I know?!' That book sold something like 4 million copies."

"I know people will want me to ask this," I said, hinting at the next question. "Do you consider yourself a redneck?"

"Yeah," he answered without hesitation. "My definition of it was always a glorious absence of sophistication. It can be temporary or permanent. The fun thing is that everybody falls into it from time to time. I'll have people come up to me at book signings and say, 'Listen, I'm not a redneck, but I've got some friends that are and. . . .' And my line is, 'Start reading the book.' They get, like, three pages in and they're admitting, 'Oh, God, I've done that!' So it's kind of fun when it includes everybody."

I probed him for his career know-how:"How did you pursue getting into the country music circuit as a comedian?"

"I just put the word out," he answered. "If anybody in country music needs an opening act, I can work clean. Then I started opening for The Judds and did some gigs with Tracy Lawrence. It just kind of happened. The country fans are probably the largest sector of my audience. I go every year to the big country-music 'Fan Fair' expo in Nashville, so when I got the record deal, it was with Warner Brothers Nashville."

As Foxworthy got more involved in the country industry, he found himself moving up the ladder of popularity—and moving from Atlanta to Los Angeles. "I really didn't want to go," he admitted. "My wife Greg insisted on it. I would send tapes to *The Tonight Show* or HBO, and they wouldn't even open them. They'd mail them back because I lived in Georgia. She kept saying, 'You're not going to know if you could've done *The Tonight Show* unless you go to L.A.' Well, she was right. I've done it twenty-nine times now."

Foxworthy and his wife made the Hollywood scene and he claims it was a wonderful time for them both. "The fun of it has been not knowing what's over the hill. And I'm really lucky. I've remained grounded and my wife's been supportive. A lot of people couldn't have lived that life-style not knowing what's coming; they like the security of knowing that a paycheck's going to be there every Friday."

Still, after two sitcoms, Foxworthy and his family decided to achieve one more goal and moved back to Atlanta. "Once in a while, Greg and I look at each other and say, 'We did it!' We always said we'd leave L.A. one day. You get out there and you see how easy it is *not* to leave. You get caught up in it. And nobody thought we'd leave," he laughed. "Everybody in L.A, talks about leaving, but a lot of them never do. Then we had kids and kept saying to ourselves, 'We're gonna leave.' And we did. Now I have a house next door to my brother and I take my kids to school every day. It's important that they have a normal life. And if I don't do a TV show, if I just do stand-up, well, I love doing stand-up."

He added: "Somebody asked me not too long ago, 'Would you ever do another TV show?' I said, 'Yeah, but they'd have to do it in Atlanta."

I asked Foxworthy about an upcoming HBO special and an album he was recording around the same time. "Well," he answered with another laugh, "I know there are some things I want to get into the special, but you know how comics are. I have to watch it, because the act is expanding so much time-wise. I have to keep it down, but keep the things I want in there."

I brought up the fact that his albums have more copies than any other comedian's, including Cosby, Pryor, and Carlin.

"I feel like it's almost irreverent to say that out loud," he replied. "When you're talking about people like Cosby and Carlin, and folks like that. Maybe when I quit doing this someday, it'll sink in. It doesn't seem real."

On the subject of writing the new album, he disclosed: "Steve Martin said one time that it took him ten years to write his first album. I thought, 'I don't know if I've got it in me to write an entire new album.' And for the first time ever, I got somebody to help me. I worked with Rich Shydner on this one. He's one of the funniest comics ever. We found the same things funny, and we really worked on it everyday. And we'd go down to the club and work on it some more."

"So you wrote the album in nine months."

"Yeah," he said proudly.

"You're not feeling the pressure of, say, a musical recording artist, who has to come up with the next big hit?" I asked.

"Well, no," he said. "I told my manager that I know I've done my work on this. If people get tired of Jeff Foxworthy, if they don't want to buy the album, I have no control over that. But the material is as good as anything I've ever done and that's very satisfying."

"A lot of comics say they'll keep doing stand-up as long as they're improving," I said, not wanting to retire this conversation.

"I think this is the best stuff I've ever done," he said sincerely. "It's like maturing a little bit, you know? I've talked to some people about that, Leno and Seinfeld, and once you start getting up around that forty age, you just learn how to do this. And I used to think when I was twenty-five: 'I know how to do this!' Well, I guess I did, but not like this."

"You're never going to quit, are you?"

"Gosh, I don't know," he answered softly. "To me, stand-up is a young person's game, and I hate more than anything seeing these people I used to love to watch now standing up there and not seeming funny anymore. I really don't want to be that person.

"My TV show was like a job," Foxworthy reflected. "I liked the people, but the process was exhausting. But stand-up's always been fun for me. I've always been a road warrior, but once you get over that millionth frequent-flyer mile, the thrill of air travel has gone. I miss my kids and my wife. But that time I'm onstage—I've always loved doing it, and I still do. That's kind of neat to find out after all these years."

17

A Taxing Career
or
No Bigger Thrill

"I love my family, but I hate family reunions. Family reunions are when you come face to face with your family tree and realize that some of the branches need to be cut."

RENÉ HICKS

Humor can come from anything, anywhere, and at almost any time. A comedian's job (and talent) is to know where to find it. The search for comedy material can sometimes rival a *Star Wars* adventure in the expanse of our galaxy covered while looking for the best joke. Then, too, it might be right in front of you just waiting to be discovered.

René Hicks has made a career out of finding the humor around her. Family, friends, a former career as a certified public accountant, and even her choice of hairstyles, have all been sources for her ever-changing material. Her natural ability to make audiences laugh has earned her appearances on most of television's favorite stand-up comedy shows, as well as guest roles in *Hangin' with Mr. Cooper* and the movie *Low Down Dirty Shame*. She's been voted College Entertainer of the Year and nominated by the American Comedy Awards as the Best Female Stand-Up.

A native of San Francisco and the daughter of a Pentecostal minister, Hicks was making a good living as a C.P.A. until the comedy bug struck. Since accountants have a reputation as serious people, I asked her where she had found the humor.

"I really didn't think of myself as being funny," she answered. "I was not the class clown, either; my parents put a large premium on education, so I couldn't act up in school. It wasn't until I was in high school and college that people would say, 'Man, you are

144

funny!' And they would wait to hear what I had to say. I would just make comments, observations. I didn't know it was funny. People would get me in trouble because they'd be laughing, but I didn't think: 'I'm going to try to say something funny.' It was never like that.

"I never *tried* to be funny, which was really the weirdest thing. I was just as amazed as anyone when people would laugh."

"Let's get back to the accounting," I said. "What's funny about that?"

"I would have accounting classes which were not only boring, but super-boring at eight o'clock in the morning. People in the class would egg me on to say funny things to liven it up. And the thing is, in those kinds of classes if you're going to say something funny it has to be within the context. It can't just be disruptive because that would be inappropriate. You'd have to find something funny about what was going on, something the instructor said, or something about the material. You know, accounting's pretty dry, but something would pop into my head.

"I also ran track and cross-country," she continued, touching on another typically unfunny activity that would have most of us crying instead of laughing. "We'd be training, running 80 to 90 miles a week, and the other distance runners would say, 'You make those runs fun!' And I'd be thinking, "Well, that's interesting."

"After college I went to a big international accounting firm, but within six months the excitement was all over for me. Not only did I hate it, but I found out that people in accounting did not like my personality. I used humor because I was in auditing and every time somebody hears 'audit,' they get scared. So I actually found that my personality helped to put them at ease. I think I was really effective, but the people I worked with—they sent us out in teams—felt I was wasting their time. I would get these reports: 'She's too friendly with the people and should be concentrating on her work'!

"The work was getting done," she explained, "but there were complaints about how I did it. But *then* they wanted me to hang out with them after work. They wanted to partake of the personality they didn't like on the job, but they wanted to hang out with me after!

"The comedy thing I just fell into," she admitted. "I'd certainly never thought about doing it for a living. Friends kept trying to talk me into it. They dared me to go onstage. They'd been going to the Holy City Zoo, in San Francisco, watching open-mike nights and were telling me I should go. I kept saying I was too busy and didn't have the time, but I did it after they dared me. I had never been in a comedy club until I went onstage. I started talking about my family, like I did at family gatherings, and that worked. People other than my friends were laughing.

"Other comics came in and said, 'You're really funny. How long have you been doing this?' I said it was my first time, and nobody believed me. They started telling me where there were other open-mike nights and other places to get onstage. Still, I didn't do a lot that first year because I was still working full

Comedian René Hicks.

time, but people would see me and ask if I wanted to MC weekend shows. I would be getting paid for it! I did comedy about six times before somebody hired me to MC a show. I could do that because it wouldn't interfere with work.

"Then I started hearing about the comedy business," she continued, "so I just started gathering information. That was the business side of me. I put together a résumé, a videotape, and business cards, and started sending them out. I thought if I could get work on the road, then I would give it a shot."

Hicks eventually took a six-month leave of absence to see how she would do on the comedy circuit. It's been almost a decade and they're still waiting for her return.

"I went on the road immediately," she remembered, "just doing weeks and weeks at a time. It didn't pay all that much, and a lot of times I had to pay my own airfare, but I used my savings and figured it was the thing to do. I went on the road because I wanted my humor to appeal to everybody. I wanted to make sure my stuff was going to be universal.

"They'd give me fifteen minutes and, material-wise, I probably had five minutes that I could do!" she laughed. "But I would just try stuff out; it was very spontaneous. That's how I started getting more material. I had a good instinct for things that are funny without having to try them out. It's tough to do the same stuff over and over, and I knew I could produce material."

"Do you look at yourself as being a comic observer?" I asked. "Do you look all around, find material, and just go with it?"

"Yes," she answered. "I'm good at picking out things that are funny. I'm really not the kind of a comic that sits all day and writes. I don't do it like that. It comes to me. I keep pieces of paper and notepads everywhere. I can observe very well, I can make up stuff on the spur of the moment, or see or hear something, and go onstage to try it, if I think it's funny.

"I go through spurts where a ton of stuff will come to me as I'm just doing things. I watch the news and I read the newspaper, and stuff comes to me. I just write it down. And that's really how my material comes about. My mind is constantly moving around all the time, and things just pop in. Sometimes I laugh, and people wonder, 'What are you laughing at?' I'll tell them, and they'll say, 'That's not funny!' And I say, 'Yes, it is!' But some of it I have to act out. I'll play the character and they'll see it's funny—I have to elaborate by doing it and showing them."

Hicks reflected on her business sense in starting out: "I think I was more successful in some ways than some comics, because I used my business background to put things together and represent myself. I'm good at talking to club owners and bookers on the phone. I think that's why I progressed more quickly than a lot of people who are funny but don't know the ins and outs. I was not only successful but less bitter about things happening or not happening, because I felt like I had more control. I know what goes on, or needs to go on.

"I think comedy is—a lot—*business*. People ignore that. They think it's all show, but it's very important to do the business part."

I asked Hicks if she thought it was harder being a woman trying to break into comedy, which has often been referred to as a boys' club.

"I come at it from a different perspective," she answered quickly. "Of course, there's a lot more guys doing comedy. And I see a lot of them, in general, who are not funny. But because there are so few women, if they're not funny they tend to stand out. I grew up with brothers, so I do a lot of sports material and have a really well-rounded act that appeals to men and women. Also to black, white, gay, straight people—across the board. That's my success and that's how I see life.

"There's a lot of women who get up and all they talk about are women's issues," she remarked, "It's boring! I've appeared onstage bald, but I never talked totally about my bald head. I would do maybe five minutes up front, to make people comfortable and get it out of the way, and spend the rest of the time just doing my act. I never wanted to have my material be just the 'bald material.' Because if I grew hair, I wouldn't have an act!"

Just for the comfort factor, I thought this might be a good place to bring up her "look," which Hicks had when she first broke into the comedy scene in Los Angeles. Back then it was rare for men to wear the bald look, but a woman with a shaved head?

"I had this short, professional-looking haircut, and my niece said I should get rid of the business look if I wanted to be a comic," she laughed. "She knew I was kind of wacky and thought I shouldn't have an accountant's hairstyle. She was into doing hair and wanted to do mine. Big mistake. She claimed the clippers slipped, but I think she just didn't like the birthday gift I got her. She cut a big gap in the middle of the hair that was on top, so I had this Three Stooges hairstyle!

"There was no way to fix it, and I had to go onstage in an hour. When it came time to decide what to do, I told her to cut it all off. It would be too ridiculous to leave it like this, and eventually it would all grow back evenly. My mother wanted me to wear a wig, and someone said I should wear a cap, but I'm pretty much who I am onstage and off. I'd rather be real, and if the cap fell off . . . ! So I went out there and made up stuff. And it worked! People were riveted by it—laughing. Other comics were saying, 'What a hook! I would never had thought of that!' And I didn't even know what a hook was! I didn't do it on purpose. They were saying, 'You've got five minutes of new material!'"

"I said, 'Oh, no, I'm growing my hair back.' But people kept saying it was incredible. I told a friend I would grow it back when it got cold, but it was the first winter of the California drought and it didn't get cold. I thought it was a sign from God because I'm very spiritual."

Since the best comedians can change with the times, Hicks never let herself be typecast as "that bald-headed black woman." When it appeared that might happen, she quickly shut the door and let the growing process begin.

"When I was bald, it made me stand out. Someone once told me that if I became the angry bald-headed black woman, I would probably get a television series. But I told them I'm not angry. I don't want to be angry. That's not who I want to be. Why can't they have a TV character who is just quirky and just looks like this? So I stayed with it, because I thought it was different. Why can't we have something just different?"

She says now that she was naïve. "People kept recognizing me by my bald head," she said. "I couldn't get away from it. People would come up to me and rub my head! It was upsetting, and after a while I didn't want people to say, 'I don't want to go see her, because she's mean.' They would have seen me on television, remember me, and think, 'I know her.'

"In this industry, if I had made it successfully as a bald person, I would have been stuck. In any role I would have had on TV, I would have been the 'bald person.'

"When I look back on that, I'm glad I didn't get a series. The attention I was already getting from being on TV with stand-up was overwhelming. To increase that by millions, I would've become like a hermit in my house. The industry tends to get locked into things, and I probably would've been stuck in a similar role, and then people would've resisted my growing my hair back.

"When I finally grew hair," she laughed, "people asked if I was afraid I was going to lose my act. I told them no, because I use the bald thing only so much. It had no effect on my comedy whatsoever."

But don't think Hicks was about to play anyone else's game by fitting into the sitcom crowd. As her hair came back, she quickly dyed it blonde.

"I thought that would be a nice transition," she pointed out. "Then after two years I went back to my real color and have been getting a lot more attention. The funny thing is that I got to show people that I can have many different looks and still get the recognition. I don't need to be blonde or bald—my personality is big enough for comedy.

"The progression of comedy has changed along with my hair," she said. "There were a lot of comedy clubs when I started, then an interest in comics doing sitcoms. But all these people who were getting many of the deals couldn't produce a funny pilot, or once they got on, they couldn't sustain the show. Now there seems to be a waning interest in having comics star in their own shows."

With her different looks and different experiences in life and the comedy industry, I asked Hicks to throw some words of wisdom our way. What advice would she give young comedians?

"Right now, comedy is more of a maverick thing, where you've got to find a way to get it done," she answered. "You really need to have that 'I'm gonna go out there and get it.' If you're sitting back and thinking it's going to come to you, more than likely it's not. You have to develop it. Use as many skills as you possibly can."

A lot of agents and managers who don't have a business background may get by on schmoozing and similar approaches, she observed. "I don't like kissing people's asses. I think you should stand on merit. Your talent should be enough. Now, there are always people who have gotten where they are by kissing ass, but the fact of the matter is, I believe you can bypass that kind of stuff with skills. With skills!

"What I would say to beginning comics is that it's a hard road. The two things you have to do are *write* and *perform*. You have to do as much of that as you possibly can. You have to persevere. You have to work very, very hard at it.

"You've also got to have a lot of confidence in yourself, and you have to be honest with yourself. You've got to be able to look at something, a situation, a bit, a joke, and say, 'This isn't working. Though I like it, it's really not working.' Because that's the only way you'll grow.

"And you have to realize that you're going to be told no more than you're going to be told yes. Even after all that, you still have to be able to sit down after you've been told no fifty times in one day and look in a mirror and say, 'It's *yes*. I know it's *yes* because I feel *yes* inside of me.' It's going to have to come from within.

"You're going to have to make some sacrifices," she advised further, giving us insight into her competitive nature. "No matter what it is—whether it's an Olympic gold medal or anything else—if you're going to be good, you'll have to make sacrifices. You'll have to determine what you're going to be able to sacrifice and how you'll be able to handle those. This is a very demanding profession, and the enthusiasm that you get from making your friends laugh has to carry you through times where you're trying to make drunk people (who don't care and don't laugh) laugh. Those are the times that you'll have to sustain yourself. So if you haven't given any thought to hard work, comedy is not the place to be.

"But it can be great," Hicks affirmed. "There's no bigger thrill than to go out and just know you've done the best set, when everything's coming together, you and the audience. There's no greater feeling in this business than when you've connected."

18 Keep Your Ears to the Streets or No One Formula for That Game

"I like to watch people get arrested. Call me sick, but that's my little hobby. But I hate to see black people get arrested because every time I walk by and a brother's getting arrested, he always looks at me like I'm supposed to help him escape."

REGGIE MCFADDEN

It doesn't seem that long ago when I first met comedian Reggie McFadden, who was just starting his comedy career in New York City. I guess time flies when you're having fun.

"I've just passed my ten-year mark in stand-up, so now I really feel like a veteran!" he told me as I mentally checked off another decade in my aging mind. "I really feel now like I know what I'm doing. Before your tenth year, you feel like you're all over the place. But after that it's like, okay, I'm pretty solid now. I know what I can do and know my capabilities."

I'm not sure he needed, or wanted, the reminder, but my first memory of McFadden was during his regular attendance at the Halls of Higher Learning—his night job working as a doorman at New York's original Improv.

"I was eighteen," he laughed, "I left that job because I was getting more work at The Comic Strip. I thought, 'I'm getting on more often over there, and I'm not even working the door!'"

Comedian Reggie McFadden's headshot pose is distinctive as well as amusing.

I reminded him that he expanded his comedy options in those early days with a car. It isn't cheap living in New York City with a car—how many stand-up comics manage that? "I still have that car!" he exclaimed. "Paid off, too."

Going for the stage experience really paid off as he rose through the club scene and into television and films. His credits include roles on *Hangin' with Mr. Cooper, Coach, Martin,* and numerous appearances on *Late Night with Conan O'Brien, The Keenan Ivory Wayans Show,* and *The Late Show with David Letterman.* He's one of the stars on Fox Television's sitcom *The Way We Work,* and also spent two years as a regular cast member on *In Living Color.*

"You know, I realized most of my sketches were with Jim Carrey," he said. "They teamed me up with Jim and Jamie Fox, mostly. That was a good learning experience. The funny thing is, I was trying to get on that show from the beginning, when they first started casting. I auditioned for *In Living Color* three times. My first audition was with David Alan Grier. He blew me away! I felt I was so out of league in that room with him, it was ridiculous! He made me laugh, and we were auditioning together! We were doing improvisations and I burst out laughing."

"Did you ever study improv?" I asked.

"Yeah! I was in an improv group and studied at Chicago City Limits in New York. I was in one for a little while when John Leguizamo had an improv group, and another with Jeff Garland, Jon Stewart, Warren Hutchinson, and Ellen Cleghorne. But everybody's schedule was too busy with stand-up and acting, so we didn't stay in it long."

"Since you've been involved in stand-up, improv, and acting," I began, leading up to a big question, "what advice would you have for people getting into this business?"

"Well, *business* is the word that should be underlined. It's definitely a business. You have to develop your art, but you also have to stay abreast of what's going on in the comedy world. You also have to set definite goals for yourself. If you want to be in film, then that's the way you should go. You should try to get film agents. Everyone's going to try to push you toward television because you're a stand-up, and you have to fight. That's a battle that you have to get over.

"Acting classes are a must," he continued. "Most stand-ups can't act. The stage is not going to make you a better actor. What it can do is make you more comfortable in front of people. Acting is a totally different art from stand-up. A lot of comics don't realize that. They think just because they can get up onstage and do a lot of different characters within the jokes, that'll suffice. When they get in front of a director and a camera—well, that's not the same thing, because you're acting *with* people.

"I was studying acting when I was working the door at The Improv," he continued. "Most of the waitresses at the club were actors, and they were telling me I should take acting classes. And I was taking classes when I first started doing stand-up. When I moved to Los Angeles, I was doing scenes and, well, auditions, too. I must have auditioned for hundreds of things. I audition for something every week. That's practice in itself!"

Since the successful businesses of acting and stand-up both require good representation, I asked him how he got his agent and manager.

"I suggest all comics pick a major city to perform in," he advised, "like Chicago, New York, Los Angeles, or even Boston. You have to go where the agents are. Mass mailings of your pictures to the agencies might work, but you have to perform in the showcase clubs. You must get into the clubs if you're going to be a stand-up, and the club owners are the people who deal with the different agencies. They set up different showcases. You have to be on their good side to be on that list. And if you're funny, the agent's going to pick you.

"If you go to New York, try to hit all the agencies and try to get everyone to come out to see you," McFadden said thoughtfully. "If that doesn't work, the next step would be a manager—one who has ties to different agencies. You have to get somebody who believes in you, and it doesn't necessarily have to be someone who's at the top of the field. I made an error with my first manager because I should have gone with someone a little bit smaller. That agency was a mega-house; it was like a factory.

"I was a new comic in Hollywood, and I didn't know the business. You should try to at least know the business side of comedy, what your purpose is, and how they're going to use you, because you're a commodity. You have to know your talents and your capabilities. If you don't, they'll be sending you up for everything like kiddie shows and PBS specials.

"Be involved with your career. That's the best thing I can say."

"As far as agents, managers, club owners and anyone else who might be important to your career," I asked, "what do you think is the best way to stay in touch with the business side of the comedy industry?"

"You have to keep your ears to the streets," he answered. "There's no scenario, no formula for that show-business game." He agreed that the best place to stay in touch is in the comedy clubs, learning what's going on, who's auditioning, or what showcases are happening. "Be there for those showcases. Carry a tape of your act, especially if you're not in that showcase. Slip it to the guy who's auditioning everybody. Just give it to him. Always carry a tape with you. And a picture. For the ones who have cars," McFadden laughed, "always keep a current tape in the car."

19 Rhodes, a Scholar of Humor or Hey, You're on Television, Right?

"Drugs have been around for a long time. I read that the Incas did drugs. I guess that explains why they were building runways for UFOs."

TOM RHODES

It's never easy to predict who will be the next major star to come from the world of comedy. Just one big break and suddenly a comedian will be off the club circuit and starring in television and movies, and only performing live in higher-priced theaters and arenas. One who seems to be fulfilling big predictions is comedian Tom Rhodes.

"I'm a wiseacre," he volunteered during a recent conversation. "I've got a comment for everything. I keep my pistols on my hips, and I'm very opinionated."

He's also one of the fastest-rising stars in the comedy industry. As the title character of NBC's 1996 sitcom *Mr. Rhodes,* he brought to network TV a youthful style of comedy that had already earned him loyal fans on Comedy Central. But don't use the term "overnight success" when referring to his career, unless you think thirteen years of paying dues in clubs throughout the country is a walk through the park.

"I started out when I was seventeen and got a fake I.D. so I could perform in the clubs around Orlando, Florida," he laughed. "I had known I wanted to be a comedian since I was twelve. When I was in my early teens, I'd go to the library and look for anything I could find on comedy, but there wasn't much available. I'd find a stray magazine article, but that was it.

"I eventually started calling clubs looking for work as an opening act," he continued. "I found one in Tulsa, Oklahoma, that would hire me, so I took off in my car. I think I was making $200 that week, and it cost me $200 to get there, so I had nothing to live on. The headliner liked me and suggested I call this club where he was playing next. I did, and they hired me, so I drove up there and did a week. That's how it started, and it was a couple of months before I got back to Florida."

During the next eleven years he laid the groundwork for a comedy persona that has him playing not only with America's current frame of mind, but also with its past. His first television special, *Viva Vietnam!*, came about because of his performances in a series of 30-second promotional spots for Comedy Central. Describing them as "like filming a rock video for a joke," they were taped in such exotic locations as jail cells and warehouses. He expounded on topics ranging from Yugoslavia to Chelsea Clinton with the cynical delivery of today's younger generation of comedians—but don't mention his being "a spokesman for Generation X."

"Generation X is here for this half-hour right now. I don't want to be Loverboy still wearing the red leather pants ten years from now," he declared. "One time I picked up a picture-postcard of Lenny Bruce and on the back it said, 'Lenny Bruce, American Comedian.' That's all I ever want to be described as: American Comedian."

The success of the promotional spots brought him Comedy Central's first-ever development deal, which turned into *Viva Vietnam!*

"I decided to go to Vietnam because it had just opened up, and my dad was over there during the war flying helicopters," he said. "You talk about all-time challenges, go to Vietnam, the ugliest thing in our history, and try to make it funny. I didn't know what the public reaction would be. I mean, are people ready? You can't get over something until you've laughed about it, and comedy is basically exaggerating your problems and your fears. I was really nervous going over there.

"The original idea for the special was to go all over the U.S. covering events," he continued. "Then we decided to do a show from Las Vegas. That didn't work out, and we got this bigger idea to go to Vietnam. It's the first Bob Hope-less comedy special ever filmed there."

Rhodes wanted the show to be a kind of "thank-you nod" for the veterans who never got anything. "I wanted to get past the Oliver Stone version, because that's all we know. Vietnam is a war, not a country, to us. It's actually a beautiful country," he remarked. Sometimes dreams and ideas don't match the finished project. I asked Rhodes if he was happy with the results.

"Yeah, I was surprised," he admitted. "There's no stand-up in the special, but there's one kind of slap at *An Evening at the Improv*. Well, it's not really a slap. There was a brick wall, and we filmed me in front of it telling one joke. It says 'Hanoi Improv' at the bottom of the screen. It's actually a slap at the brick wall.

"I got to show the finished version to my dad, and he said a very beautiful thing. He said, 'This show should offend everyone, except for veterans.' That's the only rule of thumb I wanted. They were the only people whose toes I didn't want to step on."

Viva Vietnam! was discussed and reviewed in newspapers, magazines, and on television throughout the country. As material that is "on the edge" and dangerous, it made the spotlight already shining on Rhodes a little brighter.

His involvement with Comedy Central was great for him. For one thing, people recognized him when he came to town.

"I'm not a big-shot smoking cigars," he said, "but it's nice when people come out to see you, and that's all I've ever wanted. I wish I could've stuck around Comedy Central, but the truth is, it's cable, and bigger opportunities were coming. NBC had signed me to a development deal, and we tried to find a writer and the right idea," he said. "There were a lot of bad ideas, but then the school idea of *Mr. Rhodes* came around, and I liked it. I thought of a *Dead Poets Society* where I could get a lot of my humor out. Of course, in your first year you don't have the control that Seinfeld and Rosanne have on their shows. And a lot of my humor is dangerous and edgy. How much of that can come out in a family show?

"To be honest," he chuckled, "I was learning on national television how to act, plus I had the pressure of having a show on the number-one network— although that was a dream come true. As a kid wanting to be a comedian, I would always watch NBC's Johnny Carson, and *Saturday Night Live.*"

Though *Mr. Rhodes* lasted only one season, Rhodes values the experience as another stepping-stone in his career. The role, in which he played a teacher who just happened to be hipper than his students, fit him like a glove.

"I think it got away from its original premise," he admitted, "which was a rebel against the system. I was supposed to get in trouble in the classroom every week for the revolution I was inspiring in the children. It started to slip away from that. Nonetheless, I loved it."

I asked Rhodes what plans he might have for the future.

"Well, I've always had a Steve McQueen complex. Without sounding too self-involved, I'm gonna be a movie star," he laughed. "I'm in a nice position because of the show. It amplified my wattage in terms of who I am. My agent sends me movie scripts that I'm not in a hurry to do, like a talking donkey movie or a baseball monkey movie or something like that.

"I'm a comedian first and foremost," he pointed out. "Right now, I want to be known for what I'm best at, stand-up comedy. And it's so rare when people can do it well. I mean, not that many people are comedians, first of all. It's more of a rarity when someone is really good at that, because it's a difficult and ever-changing medium. It takes a lot of work to stay on top of it. Before the sitcom, I had been going on for six nights a week for the last twelve years. Then all of a sudden, I was only doing it about every third week. I found I missed putting my own words in my mouth and writing out my own trains of thought.

"I write constantly," he added. "Short stories, long stories, and long and short jokes."

Would he go back to the sitcom world?

"That was never my primary dream. One day I'd like to go back to that world, when I'm a bigger entity in the world. You know, Bill Cosby's name has a bit more thunder than Tom Rhodes when it's on the cover of *TV Guide*.

"Everybody complains about what night they're on," he observed. "That doesn't make a bit of difference. I think they could put you on Sunday morning, and if you're someone people want to see, they'll find you."

I remarked on his balanced perspective: "I know most 'show-biz types' are usually desperate for the next break, but you're different."

He laughed, "I'm Walt Whitman! The luxury I've always had in my career is that I've never been desperate, because I was never in any hurry. Things have always been at the level they're supposed to be at. I would rather take my time, get more tuned-up on my acting skills, do independent movies, and have a smart, calculated career of quality work.

"You can never see things in desperate terms," he continued. "As a comedian in the club world, there's the ladder. I remember when I'd be an MC, and I'd say, 'Well, I'm gonna be happy just being an MC right now.' And everybody else would say, 'I've gotta middle and I've gotta headline! I've gotta do this and that. . . !' Everybody's so frantic when they don't enjoy where they are right now, you know?"

"You're just a down-to-earth guy," I said with a bit of envy, "which can be a bit rare in the entertainment industry. What are the crowds like that are coming to see you now?"

"There are people who come out thinking they're going to see the nice teacher-man—which is fine, but I am a live comedian first and foremost, and I think the power of expression is everything. I like to—like you said—step on people's toes. It's great.

"There are also the people who've been watching me for years. It's always funny when they come up to me and mention a joke I did on some ancient stand-up show. Or something that I don't do anymore, things I've forgotten, but they make me proud."

Since Rhodes is a thriving member of the new generation of comedians, I wondered what advice he would have for the next.

"It's a lonely life. Study the masters, and stick with it no matter how ragged and broke you get, which will happen many times," he said. "Do whatever you can to get onstage. Kill if you have to. Driving 200 miles to do a set should not stop anyone serious about this business from performing.

"I don't think there are enough comedians. There aren't enough people bringing goodness into the world. Anybody who can make people forget about their problems is kind of a healer."

Healer, writer, actor, chaser of ghosts from America's past—with so much going on, I asked what audiences can expect from Tom Rhodes in the future.

"Steaming plates of hot emotion!" he answered.

20

A Picture Is Worth a Million Words, or Help Me, Rhonda!

"My boyfriend just turned forty, but one thing you guys never have to worry about when you turn forty is losing your hair. Because men never really lose their hair. It just starts growing into their scalp and out their nose and ears."

RHONDA SHEAR

Rhonda Shear has had a few titles in her career, including comedian, actor, and beauty-pageant winner. Fans of Friday-night television should immediately recognize her from the popular movie-fest *U.S.A.: Up All Night,* in which she introduces films, interviews guests, and, most importantly, performs comedy sketches during much-anticipated commercial breaks. Her program's Rhonda character has been described as a combination of Jayne Mansfield and Lucille Ball, but carries the original stamp of its star through her satire and sarcastic brand of humor.

Rhonda (the original) is a native of New Orleans. A former Miss Louisiana, she has a degree in marketing and communications from Loyola University. After a near-miss run for political office in her home state, she moved to Los Angeles to conquer the world of comedy and acting. With credits that include sitcoms, films, and headline shows in clubs, theaters, and casinos, she's done very well.

"I still have *Up All Night* on the air and another show on syndication," she told me after I asked how things were going. "The stand-up is probably the best it's ever been. Of course, I only want to work in cities where there's a Neiman-Marcus or Saks. It's in my contract rider. I actually know cities by their malls."

After a good laugh and an accurate description of my local mall, Shear explained that she'd gone to California to pursue her interest in comedic acting. But sometimes people are too quick to judge a book by its cover. "I have a strange background of being, you know, bigger than life," she said. "Southern girls with big hair, big butts, big boobs, big Mardi Gras beads, big everything! I wanted to do comedy, but I was a former Miss Louisiana and people said, 'Oh no, you can't be a comedian. You don't look like a comedian.' Sexy and funny just don't mix to most people. You can be pretty and perky, but you

Comedian Rhonda Shear.

can't have a sexy look—and, well, that's just the way I'm built. So I tried everything else in between.

"I was in a comedy improvisational class, and I met a guy named Kenny Ellis. We started a comedy act that was improv, sketch comedy, mime, and whatever else we thought was funny," she remembered. "We used to crash people's offices. At the time, Johnny Carson was on the air, and we crashed his producer's office, and he actually let us do our five-minute piece. It was a kooky little act. And we wound up crashing Dick Clark's office, and he put us on the air during a special.

"After my act with Kenny disbanded, I got back into acting," she continued. "I was dating comedian Bobby Kelton and just hanging with him at the clubs. I started getting that yen again. I remember one day announcing to him, 'I'm a stand-up comic,' and I went out and did one of those showcase rooms. I followed five little kids doing Michael Jackson and thought I was gonna throw up. I got, I think, one laugh, and someone sneezed in the back, and I was hooked. I started working like crazy. I was writing and, just because of my look, I was getting hired to MC. It was costing me more to get to these gigs, but I was working the good clubs.

"I worked in Las Vegas at Catch a Rising Star, I swear, it couldn't have been six months after I said my first words onstage alone. One night the headliner overslept, and I thought, 'Oh, my God, I have like five minutes of material!' But Jon Stewart was the feature act, and we played onstage together, and it was a very special night."

"Did you find being a woman made it easier for you in comedy?" I asked.

"Harder!" she answered firmly. "I remember going to a showcase, and all the guys were sitting around and flirting with me. We were all starting around the same time and they were, like, kidding me. I went onstage and got laughs, and when I got back to the table where they were all sitting, no one would talk to me. Guys will sit around and give each other lines and help each other. Maybe a couple of guys on the road through the years has said to me, 'You know, I think this line may work better. . . .'

"I did have a rough time as a woman. It was a little scary, too. Having a certain look had me watching over my shoulder when I left clubs. It was sometimes great and sometimes a little scary, but I didn't have anything horrendous happen to me.

"It's more of a male-oriented business. You never laugh at Mom you know? You always laugh at Dad, because he's the one who does goofy things with the kids. And women have a softer voice quality, in general. I've done the exact same jokes a male has done onstage and the men get a bigger laugh. It just has to do with the sound of our delivery. So I think women have it just a little bit rougher, along with other business obstacles.

"But I like the fact that I went on the road and worked in all these horrible places and would drive to barrooms where nobody was listening. If they don't pay cover charges, they don't listen. That's why I used to say, 'Just make them pay two dollars. If they pay, they will listen.' But it made me a better performer. So I recommend that people do that, not just say, 'I'm gonna work the big clubs and get a sitcom tomorrow.' You'll get your sitcom, but the experience of the road is invaluable; it does teach you. I still work the road, but I try to do it on a different level now."

Since comedy is a business, I asked Shear for her thoughts on her promotional photos, bios, and videos. Did she have a handle on this even in her early career?

"Yes," she answered, "it comes from my acting and my background, which says you have to spend money to make money. Spend some money on your 'press,' and do not keep using the same photo you've had for years. Have a bunch of different shots. I believe that anytime you have a gig on the road, you should do everything you can. Call a newspaper. What's great about getting press in a newspaper if you're working in a club is that if they like the artwork, they'll run the photo. And a picture is worth a million words.

"The business can be really tough," she admitted. "Bookers can be intimidating, but you have to do your thing. If they want you to come in early and do radio and other promotions, you have to do it. It's good for your experience in being able to spar with the deejays. Also, for your own timing, it's great. I think you're only helping yourself.

"Self-promoting is really important," she asserted, "because this *is* a business, and so few people make it and survive on just doing stand-up. Who knows what other doors will open? I figure, just do it all."

"You don't just throw it into the hands of an agent or manager?" I pried.

"No," she answered. "As a matter of fact, that drives managers crazy; they don't feel I give up enough to let them do what they do. And they're probably right. Because I have been hands-on in my own career for a long time, it's hard for me to just trust someone. I don't want someone to turn down something because he or she doesn't think it's right for me. I want to be there. I want to know what's going on.

"Joan Rivers is my idol," she remarked, "and I love what she does and the fact that she sells things on the air, does movies, does hosting . . . Nothing precludes her from doing all this stuff. "

Shear's knowledge of public relations has kept her working and growing as an act throughout her career. She also added to her stage time and that of other women comedians during her earlier years by promoting *Babes of Comedy* shows every Monday at The Laugh Factory in Los Angeles. The idea is to get onstage as often as possible and the audience will tell you the rest.

"A lot of people ask, 'How will I know if I'm funny?' You'll know when you walk onstage. You'll know if you're funny, and if you like it or hate it, and if you get stage fright.

"A friend of mine wanted to do stand-up, so he got up and told these stories that I definitely thought were wrong for him. But listen, who am I to say? It's subjective. If it works for him, then it works. There's no right or wrong in comedy. I feel if you're getting laughs, then that's working. I've known comedy snobs, where if it's not intellectual . . . ," she began, and broke into a laugh. "Hey, we're not doing Shakespeare here. We're making people laugh! Whatever works, it's just making people forget where they are in their lives and making them feel good. My style isn't cerebral, and I'm glad it's not. It's who I am and it's coming from reality."

"The idea, then, is to be original and creative," I said, "both onstage and off."

"Right. No matter what other comics try to intimidate you into," she laughed.

With her television shows, radio appearances, and live performances, it seems as if Shear must stay up all night *and* all day working. Is that a schedule most comics follow to improve their careers and their acts?

"You have to do that," she agreed, "but sometimes you can become obsessed with it, and you have to relax. I see these guys who bring their computers on the road with them, and that's good. I've gotten one and I've tried to do that. But then I've just decided, 'No. I'm gonna go out! I'm in Boston, I'm gonna have some fun!' You know, just being in Boston and doing something goofy becomes material anyway.

"Again, there are no rules, and that works for me. I'm a less disciplined person by nature, even when I'm doing *Up All Night*. I'm not one to rehearse, rehearse, rehearse. And other people are. Different things work for different folks.

"There are comics, I thought, who improvised a lot of their stuff," she continued, "but some of them are organized onstage and just know what they're doing. I'm up there, not winging it, but I'll try things that pop into my head."

I asked Shear what words she might have for comics just getting into the business. If she were writing her "Help Me, Rhonda" advice column, what would be the answer?

She stated: "Don't let anyone discourage you, because everyone will *try* to, especially in comedy. There is more negativity there than in any other business. Just do your own thing. Get that stage time no matter how laborious, no matter how far the drive may be. It will be worth it. If you really love it, you'll stick with it. Once the comedy bug bites, it's hard to get away from it."

21

The Adjustment Was Minor or That's What I Enjoy Most

"I just bought a leather couch. They should tell you that, when it's warm and you sit on a leather couch in your underwear, when you stand up the whole couch comes with you."

RONDELL SHERIDAN

During the 1995–96 television season, NBC premiered a sitcom called *Minor Adjustments* that wound up breaking new ground in the prime-time scheduling routine. In late December, the series went off the air but was immediately picked up by the upstart UPN Network, which began broadcasting new episodes the following month. This marked the first time a weekly series switched networks in the same season.

Though it became a bit of a chore for fans to follow *Minor Adjustments,* because of the changes in time and network, star Rondell Sheridan gained recognition in households across the nation. As Dr. Ron Aimes, a child psychologist of the '90s, he was the lone voice of sanity among his co-workers, family, and friends.

Unfortunately, with so many adjustments being made to *Minor Adjustments,* the sitcom was not renewed for the following season. Sheridan's Dr. Aimes is now officially retired, but there's no reason to feel bad for this gifted comedian from Chicago's South Side. He seems to thrive on change. In fact, it wasn't long after that he moved

Comedian Rondell Sheridan.

into another series, *Uncle Skeeter,* on the Nickelodeon network.

I first met Sheridan when I did bookings at the New York Improv in the late 1980s. He was one of the most sought-after acts in that city and was gaining a lot of attention from the Los Angeles entertainment industry, too. It always guaranteed a great show when he would call in to say he was available to perform at the club.

I called him at his home in Los Angeles for his reflections and advice for comics. The three-hour time difference from the East Coast made this a wake-up call, but he shook off all signs of sleep, and the only thing I missed were the lively facial expressions that are a mainstay of his live shows.

"Whenever you called in," I said, reminding him of his early New York days, "club bookers knew they would have a good show."

"Trust me," he laughed. "It took many years before that happened!"

A graduate of Marquette University with a degree in advertising and marketing, Sheridan moved to New York to pursue a career as an actor. He joined a prestigious acting school, the Circle in the Square, and performed in off-Broadway productions and, elsewhere, in many regional theaters.

"At Circle in the Square," he remembered, "I got started doing stand-up because a classmate's sister was a stand-up. I started hanging out with her. The first club I went to was, I think, Mostly Magic. It was also the first club where I did stand-up. I think I only did it three times before I passed the audition at the Improv."

"Really?" I replied, thinking of the acts who'd needed to go through that pressure-cooker more than a few times to make it onto the Improv's roster.

"Yeah, I always had a good gift for ad-libbing, and a couple of things happened in the audience during my audition. Plus, I dressed up, and none of the other comics dressed up for the audition. I sort of looked like I'd been doing this for a long time.

"When I think back on what I did, there was really nothing there except a couple of completely unplanned lines about things that happened, and they were just seamless. If I had been doing it a little bit longer, I probably would have never done it the way I did—I would have been afraid to! But when you've never done something before, you don't have that fear, and you just go with it. And that was it. I went to a few other clubs, but I got really lucky and found a great home at the Improv.

"I look at comics who are just starting now," he continued, "and they've got no sense of how to do it except from watching television. All their peers are pretty much at the same level as they are. I grew up watching Seinfeld, Reiser, Leifer, Siskind, Belzer . . . and I got to see a wealth of comics. It was a good foundation to begin with."

"Was anybody more of an influence than others?" I asked.

"Cosby, specifically," he answered quickly, "I don't do it as much anymore, but I do have some standard bits that are in a story form. And Carlin. And Pryor is one of the best physical comics we've ever had.

"I never thought I was going to be a stand-up," he said thoughtfully. "I was always a comedy fan. My influences were all on TV—Flip Wilson, the Smothers Brothers, all those guys. When I had to figure out what I wanted to do, there was a comic named Mike Langworthy, who's a writer and producer now, and I used to ask him, 'How do you put all the jokes together?' I was really asking him how you do a bit, how you get a bit together. He said, 'You get all your jokes that are on one topic, or you get some kind of theme so they're all together, and you work it from there.' I said, 'Well, I want to do stories.' He had seen the story I was working on and he said, 'It really wasn't a story. It was just a re-e-e-eally lo-o-o-ong joke.'

"So I asked him, 'What do you mean? Cosby does stories.' He said, 'No, let me tell you what the difference is. Cosby tells a really long story, and in it there are a lot of jokes. You told one joke that was re-e-e-eally lo-o-ong.'

"I thought, 'Ohhh! I'm beginning to see now!'"

"It's hard," Sheridan went on. "I begin with one moment that's really funny, and I just begin to pull it apart more and more to get more specific and get more jokes. By the time I've got about three or four jokes in a story, then I can pretty much bring it onstage and try to work it out and keep embellishing it until I get the whole thing.

"Still, I begin the same way, with one really long joke. But now, normally, the joke is really funny, and then everything around it is funny. It's hard, because the way I do it, if I do it as a joke it doesn't work. I have to do it in a story form for it to work."

"You keep all your material pretty much family oriented," I said.

"Since I've gotten a little older and more comfortable with myself," he answered, "I'm becoming closer to *me*. Now my shows have become a little looser. People still come up to me and say, 'You know, it's such a clean show, it's so refreshing.' But I think when I do curse, and it's not the 'biggies,' it's so conversational and rare you don't even notice it.

With *Minor Adjustments* off the air, I wondered if there were any future prime-time projects. Sheridan began talking excitedly about his television work. "We're trying to see if we can get into a development deal. I have options on a couple of shows. It's weird, because the first time I did it, I don't think I realized how difficult it is to do everything that I did. There was a point where I thought, 'Wait a minute. Nobody has it this easy doing all this.' But it all went pretty smooth, without a hitch. It was the first time I had pitched a show. I went to the network, the first network we went to, they liked it, and we got the money for the pilot. They approved the script, we did the pilot and got picked up.

"I'm almost positive that was the first time a TV show moved from one network to another in the same calendar year. I can't recall any other show doing that. There might have been, but we searched high and low and didn't come up with one. Getting cancelled in December and being off the air for maybe six weeks, and *boom*, back on in January. It was fantastic that it happened. So I definitely got the bug. I'm thinking, 'Man, I want to do this! I want to go to syndication!' Right now I'm thinking it.

"I told Drew Carey this," he continued, "And it's funny, I had no comparisons—I'd seen shows taped, but I don't think I had ever seen a pilot taped. And we had tons of good people around our show, but I'm curious, I want to see what the competition's like. So I went to see a gazillion pilots. I saw Drew's show, and I swore it was *the* funniest show (it was just hilarious) and I was jealous. It was like Drew wrote his own script, and I was saying, 'Damn!'

"But I kept thinking, 'You know what, Rondell? You're just not ready to write your own script yet.' I can get the story, and I can get the characters but it's a different feel to it. So I got hooked up with Ken Estin who did *Taxi, Cheers,* and Tracy Ullman's show. He was a great ensemble writer. NBC was really high on him. So we retooled the show and put a few little changes in it, and *bam!*

"It was a long process," he emphasized. "We began in September of 1994 with the basic idea. NBC said, 'Yeah, here's the money. Go do the script.' And we went until about April 1995, when we shot the pilot. So we had tons of meetings, rewrites, everything. It's really a much longer process when I stop and think about it. From the time we began to the time we aired was more than a year.

"Some shows get on really quick," he went on. "And it doesn't necessarily mean it's a midseason replacement. It means you can get the ball rolling for a show in February and pound out that script fast. We had the really great fortune of being able to sit back and do a complete storyboard on just about everything. Because by the time I saw the first draft of the first script, I remember looking at it and thinking, 'This is exactly what we were talking about.' There were no surprises in it, but we'd spent three months doing a storyboard on it and talked about all the dialogue that was going to happen."

From the tone in his voice, I knew it was no great exaggeration to comment on how much he seemed to enjoy the whole experience.

"Yeah, I did," he agreed. "It was scary, because as an actor you're never allowed to be on 'the other side.' I mean, there *I* was, in on casting. I was there on everything. At every point while I was there, I was always afraid somebody was going to look at me and go, 'Uh, Rondell, you have to leave now.' I was never used to being on the other side of the door! They'd close the door and I'm the people talking about the person! See, as an actor, I would be outside saying, 'Gee, I wonder if they like me?'

"That taught me a lot about auditioning, because I got to see some actors come in and just nail something. I also got to see other people who weren't prepared. It was fantastic."

"Like going to school?" I asked.

"The experience I got that year . . . even if I was an apprentice and just starting out in this business, I wouldn't have gotten the experience I got in that year. It would have been maybe three years down the line."

"How about some advice for young comedians looking to get into your position?" I asked, not meaning to imply that he could ever be replaced.

"Just keep working. I used to tell young comics a long time ago to work clean. Work clean if you want to make it. But then I changed my tone; I started looking around and said, 'You know, I could never have given that advice to a Martin Lawrence. Because that's not who Martin Lawrence is. That's not his style.'

"I've rephrased it now to say, 'Be who you are.' Unless you're going to play some character. If you're pretty much walking onstage as who you are, be that person. Be that person who makes the people around you laugh. If you curse, then that's what you do. That's how you work. You couldn't start an art school and tell everyone to stay in the line because Picasso and Monet would say, 'Wait a minute! We do something else completely different!'

"So my advice is just to be true to yourself and work. And see as much live comedy as you can see. Television is like a fraud, as far as what comedy is. It's like people who listen to records and have never been to a live concert. Then they finally go to a live concert and they're blown away ('Wow, this is incredible!') It's, like, the energy it has.

"And comedy is even more special," Sheridan concluded, "because you know it's in that moment. Especially if you get someone who's very glib and ad-libs, you know it came right from the top. It wasn't rehearsed! Those people watching aren't being paid! That's what I enjoy the most."

22 Two for the Road, or Always Keep 'Em Guessing

Tommy: *"Take that back."*

Dick: *"No."*

Tommy: *"Here's fifty bucks to apologize."*

Dick: *"That's disgusting. That is a bribe."*

Tommy: *"No, it's not. It's a contribution."*

THE SMOTHERS BROTHERS

Performing as a successful comedy team is not as easy as some of the greats have made it look. You can't just throw any Tom, Dick, or Harry onstage . . . Wait, let's rephrase that thought.

If it's the right Tom and Dick, as in the Smothers Brothers, then you are talking about one of the most successful duos in comedy history. The brothers have been in show business for forty years, which means their career has surpassed all other comedy teams in history.

"The Smothers Brothers have been together longer than any other comedy team as far as years go," said Tommy Smothers. "When you see a team like Laurel and Hardy and watch their films, they live on forever. But their actual time together, along with Martin and Lewis . . . Well, no one's worked as long as we have together."

Tom (the guitar-playing comedian) and his brother Dick (the bass-playing straight man) were an in-demand comedy duo long before they ruffled the feathers of network television executives in the late 1960s by airing their political views weekly to a nation that was being torn apart by the Vietnam War. When it came to keeping audiences tuned in and wondering what they might dare say next, the stars of *The Smothers Brothers Comedy Hour* became prime-time's version of Lewis and Clark by exploring the limits of censorship as no one had before.

The sons of a West Point graduate, Tom and Dick were "army brats" who followed their parents to various military bases before settling in Southern California. Tommy began his comedy career hosting high school assemblies, and Dick sang in the school choir. While both were attending college at San Jose State, they formed

Tommy Smothers in his dressing room at the State Theatre, Sandusky, Ohio.

a folk music group and slowly watched their act develop into a comedy team. After numerous headline shows and comedy albums, the brothers were cast as the stars of a short-lived sitcom in 1966, *The Smothers Brothers Show.*

"We were stars before we were competent," laughed Tommy. "We'd been in the business only about five years and we got a television show that took away our guitar and bass. We did it like a movie."

Their next small-screen project, *The Smothers Brothers Comedy Hour,* proved they were finally ready for stardom and became a ground-breaking show. They led the way for many shows that, today, make the Smothers' style seem tame.

"Mason Williams was one of our writers," Tommy said. "He wrote 'Classical Gas,' which was 1968's number-one song. He was an old folk buddy and pretty much was kind of a morals-setter for us. That kept the show on its feet. We had Steve Martin, Rob Reiner, Johnny Hartford, and a whole bunch of writers. I got to bring on these guys that I liked, and I pretty much had creative control on the show."

Thinking back to the Sunday nights spent watching their *Comedy Hour,* I mentioned one comedy bit that would definitely fit the "unpredictable" category. Tommy grew a mustache for at least part of a season.

"Dickie came back the second year with a mustache and longer hair," he reminisced. "I said, 'God, his hair's curly, and he's got a mustache. I'll grow one, too.' So I came back—I think it was the third year—with a mustache and had it on for three shows. I think I was getting too serious, and I thought the mustache was making me unfunny. So I told a lie, and Dickie said, 'You don't deserve that . . .' and he pulled off my buttons, with a drum roll. Then he ripped off the mustache. No one in the audience knew they'd shaved mine off and put this special one on—only the director and the hair guy who had a special mustache made for me knew. So it got an incredible response when he reached up and pulled it off."

I pointed out that the show was never cancelled. The brothers were fired.

"That's very important," he laughed. "We were fired for our stand on Vietnam, basically."

"How did you feel when you were fired?" I asked.

"I was pissed!" he answered. "It took me about four years to get over it. We stopped working in the early '70s because we were blackballed. We were just kind of a dead issue. We were having trouble getting eye contact with our peers."

I asked if he still carried any hard feelings toward the network. He answered, "No, it's over. You have to maintain a perspective, and I got too close to it. I forgot my satire and became an advocate. Pat Paulsen stayed real clear about what he was doing, and I got involved in issues and a little harsh." Still, the brothers got out their message, which also included an appearance by Tommy on John Lennon's anthem, "Give Peace a Chance."

After the demise of the *Comedy Hour*, Tommy Smothers performed in dinner theaters and as a solo stand-up comedian before officially reuniting with his brother. They performed for a year on Broadway in the show *I Love My Wife*, then took it on a national tour for six months. Club dates followed which led to another radical meeting with Lennon, this time with different results.

"I had been hanging around with Harry Nilsson and working on stand-up material by myself," he said. "It was in the early '70s, and I was in New York doing a show at the Cellar Door. I got there, and they told me some guy named Harry Nilsson says he's here and wants a ticket. I had just left him in Los Angeles, but he had flown out on his own. Well, I bombed something terrible. I had about an hour of material that I went through in about 20 minutes. My timing was off. I had to do two shows a night for a week, and the first two nights Harry was up in the balcony. I asked some questions and the audience would respond. Pretty soon he started heckling, and the shows got pretty funny.

"About two months later," he continued, "we were playing at The Troubadour, in Los Angeles, and Harry called John Lennon and said, 'Tom loves to be heckled. You gotta save him.' So they came in all juiced-up and they got pretty vulgar. So it turned into kind of a mini-riot. We all got over it, but it was pretty exciting. I think it was '73 or '74."

Looking back on their career, the Smothers Brothers have always been an act that keeps audiences guessing what they're going to come out with next. Tom especially seems to say whatever is on his mind.

"On our television show and in that environment there was a tendency to want to be as current as possible and have a political point of view, with the heat of the Vietnam War and everything. If someone asked me if I think I changed the face of television, I'd say no, no, no! But if I had been asked five years after it, I would have had a totally different viewpoint as far as what the show accomplished. But as you get further away, you see it in another perspective. It's just softer. I don't think I did anything more exceptional than anybody else would've done under the circumstances. At the time, though, I was a pretty arrogant, assertive guy.

"Now we have a vague structure that we lay our show on," he said. "But we improv a lot. There's always the opening piece, which is totally improvisational, then we move through the show almost like jazz musicians. We can do chord inversions, verbally change things around, and there's always something that we'll throw in to keep our own interests alive. The show's real solid. It's probably some of our best work. Everyone expects the Smothers Brothers to be good, and they're not disappointed—I can say that, it's not ego. Our show now is not nearly as political as it was when we had the television show. Times have changed."

"Have you changed?" I interrupted.

"Oh, I'm still pissed off!" he chuckled. "I'm just as disgusted with the things going on in this country. Nobody seems to care about the money coming in and buying the White House and all that stuff.

"In a two-man comedy show, it's a little more difficult to be a Mort Sahl or Jackie Mason. We have some social observations and some pretty good generalizations, but they're not specific—we don't name names."

"So you're still political," I offered.

"There's still an attitude," he answered.

"People who haven't seen us live and only know us from television," he continued, "are impressed with the musical side of the act. Michael Preddy, whom we call our Authorized Piano Player, has been with us about sixteen years. It's like having another straight man or comedian. I get it from my brother, and I get it from Michael. We still use the bass and guitar, and we also have a trio that travels with us. The music is very good. It's pretty eclectic, what we do—a little Broadway, a little folk. . . . "

But there's more to a Smothers Brothers show than the duo and their musicians. Billing always includes the Yo-Yo Man. Is that really Tommy Smothers?

"We've always been vaudevillians at heart," he laughed. "Yo-Yo Man is a big part of it. He's the closing of the show. We talk about him as a third person. He wears a different suit and has a song. Dickie works as the play-by-play announcer for the yo-yo tricks because I don't make 'em work all the time: 'He's out of the groove! Come on Yo-Yo Man, get with it!'"

The Smothers Brothers still do 75 to 100 performances each year, but as the father of a son and daughter, Tommy enjoys focusing attention on his family. Their schedule is planned around certain holidays, and he admits that at this point in life, they don't have to work so hard.

"Dick and I have talked it over," he said. "I truly think he's one of the great straight men in comedy-team history. He's really solid. You know, if the audience does not believe the straight man, they don't believe the comedian. Comedy teams were always successful—you know, they used to be very popular and the thing to do—but every one of the straight men was exceptional. If you have a really exceptional comic and a poor straight man, it's not going to work. Dan Rowan was very good with Dick Martin. The audience looks at the straight man, maybe it's unconscious, and Dan was an exceptional straight man. Even if the comic's doing outrageous things, saying stupid things, if the straight man believes it, the audience goes along with it. Dick is that kind of guy.

"We've talked about how long we'll keep doing it," he continued. "As long as people are showing up to see the shows and we're having fun doing them, then we'll continue doing it. So comedians don't just die, they kind of fade away."

When it comes to a signature line, it's hard to beat Tommy's "Mom always liked you best!"

"It's a classic, isn't it?" he agreed, laughing.

"It is a classic. I don't think anyone who's a fan of comedy can say it anymore without thinking of you."

"We don't even use it in the show, because two middle-aged men arguing about who Mom liked best doesn't read so well. But we do introduce ourselves with the voiceover announcement as we come onstage: 'Welcome to the stage Mother Smothers' favorite son . . . *and* the other one.' So we touch on it for a moment."

According to show-business legend, Tom and Dick were never the poster boys for a brotherly love relationship. There have always been plenty of rumors about the siblings not getting along. I asked how they did it.

"It's, uh, therapy and operation," he answered mischievously.

"A big rumor was that you stopped working together because of an argument," I said, pushing the point. "We heard you weren't getting along."

"That wasn't the problem," he explained. "The problem was that I wasn't funny anymore. I had about three years of not being funny. I was very involved in the issues of being cancelled and censorship and all that kind of stuff. It's a tenuous relationship. Dick says it's like an old marriage—lots of fighting and no sex. But we've gone to a counselor so that we could work better. We're notorious for having disagreements. Our arguments are real. Our differences are profound. We go onstage, and we don't have to fake our positions. He is a pragmatist, everything is black and white, and my character both on- and offstage is more emotional and spontaneous. So that works perfectly for a comedian and a straight man. As Dickie says, we worked out our differences a long time ago, and we'll work 'em out again tomorrow. That keeps it fresh for us and is also one of the reasons, I guess, that there's not so many comedy teams anymore. It takes a lot of adjustment and understanding on each part. On each person's."

"How do you work out your routines?" I asked. "Onstage?"

"We talk them over, then we go onstage and take the risk and see how they run," he said. "We can walk out there with nothing prepared and definitely get into a routine.

"Generally, we make an outline: 'Let's talk about this or that and see where it goes.' Invariably, audience attention will discover our jokes for us. And we don't tell many jokes. They're mostly attitude. Except for 'Mom always liked you best,' 'Oh yeah?!' Otherwise, I don't think we're noted for any particular joke."

I commented, "You opened a lot of doors for people who followed you."

"Yeah, that's the way it played out," he agreed. "I did an interview once, and Bob Einstein, who is Super Dave and played Officer Judy on our show, called and said, 'How come you're always talking about the past?' I said *I* don't bring it up. Bob said, 'The guys think you passed away or something!' I try to make the point that it was over thirty years ago that we had that show and people still go back to it. Some people thought we were fired because we were talking dirty."

"The Rolling Stones have fans from the old days, but are earning new ones by still recording and touring. That's how I look at The Smothers Brothers," I said.

"Dick and I have changed the act. It's more sophisticated now because we're more sophisticated as people. We have more life under our belts. And it's much more interesting, actually, than it was when we first started. The Smothers Brothers involves spirit as well as attitude, and we believe in the spaces in between," he said. "The silence. It's just like music. It's not the notes so much as where the silences are put. Laurel and Hardy had it. Bob Newhart has it. That place where today's comics are filling every space with words. What we do, it's a little more old-fashioned, but we thrive on the silence. The long take, the look. An unfunny sentence will become funny if the *timing* is done right. That's one of the reasons that we've succeeded, I think, besides being brothers.

"If you're not funny, it doesn't matter what they think about you. If you don't have it onstage, it doesn't sustain a career. We owe it to our patience with the silences and thoughts in between, without the words."

Index

About the Author

DAVE SCHWENSEN has extensive experience in the comedy and entertainment industry in New York, Los Angeles, and Cleveland. He has been the talent coordinator for *A&E's An Evening at the Improv*, and for the famous Improv clubs in New York and Los Angeles. At the latter club, he was the assistant to Budd Friedman. Dave also worked as a talent adviser for many New York and Los Angeles—based comedy programs, television networks, and film studios. As a performer he has appeared in theatrical productions, soap operas, commercials, films, radio jingles, and, of course, comedy clubs. The owner of Dave Schwensen Entertainment, he books talent for clubs, colleges, corporate shows, concerts, theaters, and special events. A teacher of comedy workshops, Dave is a freelance entertainment writer and an award-winning humor columnist. As a motivational humorist, he speaks to businesses, schools, and organizations about the value of humor as a stress relief and to build professional and personal relationships. A graduate of Bowling Green State University, he lives in northern Ohio, with his wife Debbie and their sons Kevin and Paul. For more information, visit www.thecomedybook.com and www.davelaughs.com